Notes

Estimates of the effect on employment of the options to increase the minimum wage are rounded to the nearest 100,000 workers.

Numbers in the text, tables, and figures may not add up to totals because of rounding.

Contents

The Effects of a Minimum-Wage Increase on Employment and Family Income

Summary

Increasing the minimum wage would have two principal effects on low-wage workers. Most of them would receive higher pay that would increase their family's income, and some of those families would see their income rise above the federal poverty threshold. But some jobs for low-wage workers would probably be eliminated, the income of most workers who became jobless would fall substantially, and the share of low-wage workers who were employed would probably fall slightly.

What Options for Increasing the Minimum Wage Did CBO Examine?

For this report, the Congressional Budget Office (CBO) examined the effects on employment and family income of two options for increasing the federal minimum wage:

■ A "$10.10 option" would increase the federal minimum wage from its current rate of $7.25 per hour to $10.10 per hour in three steps—in 2014, 2015, and 2016. After reaching $10.10 in 2016, the minimum wage would be adjusted annually for inflation as measured by the consumer price index.

■ A "$9.00 option" would raise the federal minimum wage from $7.25 per hour to $9.00 per hour in two steps—in 2015 and 2016. After reaching $9.00 in 2016, the minimum wage would not be subsequently adjusted for inflation.

What Effects Would Those Options Have?

The $10.10 option would have substantially larger effects on employment and income than the $9.00 option would—because more workers would see their wages rise; the change in their wages would be greater; and, CBO expects, employment would be more responsive to a minimum-wage increase that was larger and was subsequently adjusted for inflation. The net effect of either option on the federal budget would probably be small.

Effects of the $10.10 Option on Employment and Income. Once fully implemented in the second half of 2016, the $10.10 option would reduce total employment by about 500,000 workers, or 0.3 percent, CBO projects. As with any such estimates, however, the actual losses could be smaller or larger; in CBO's assessment, there is about a two-thirds chance that the effect would be in the range between a very slight reduction in employment and a reduction in employment of 1.0 million workers (see Table 1).

Many more low-wage workers would see an increase in their earnings. Of those workers who will earn up to $10.10 under current law, most—about 16.5 million, according to CBO's estimates—would have higher earnings during an average week in the second half of 2016 if the $10.10 option was implemented.[1] Some of the people earning slightly more than $10.10 would also have higher earnings under that option, for reasons discussed below. Further, a few higher-wage workers would owe their jobs and increased earnings to the heightened demand for goods and services that would result from the minimum-wage increase.

---

1. In addition to the people who became jobless, some workers earning less than $10.10 per hour and not covered by minimum-wage laws would also not have increased earnings.

Table 1.

Estimated Effects on Employment, Income, and Poverty of an Increase in the Federal Minimum Wage, Second Half of 2016

	$10.10 Option[a]	$9.00 Option[b]
Change in Employment		
Central estimate[c]	-500,000 workers	-100,000 workers
Likely range[d]	Very slight decrease to -1.0 million workers	Very slight increase to -200,000 workers
Number of Workers With Hourly Wages Less Than the Proposed Minimum Whose Earnings Would Increase in an Average Week[e]	16.5 million	7.6 million
Change in Real Income (2013 dollars, annualized)[f]		
Families whose income is below the poverty threshold	$5 billion	$1 billion
Families whose income is between one and three times the poverty threshold	$12 billion	$3 billion
Families whose income is between three and six times the poverty threshold	$2 billion	$1 billion
Families whose income is six times the poverty threshold or more	-$17 billion	-$4 billion
Change in the Number of People Below the Poverty Threshold[g]	-900,000	-300,000

Source: Congressional Budget Office based on monthly and annual data from the Census Bureau's Current Population Survey.

a. The minimum wage would rise (in three steps, starting in 2014) to $10.10 by July 1, 2016, and then be indexed to inflation.

b. The minimum wage would rise (in two steps, starting in 2015) to $9.00 by July 1, 2016, and would not be subsequently indexed to inflation.

c. Uses values at or near the midpoints of estimated ranges for key inputs.

d. In CBO's assessment, there is a two-thirds chance that the actual effect would be within this range.

e. Some of the people with hourly wages slightly above the proposed minimum wage would also have increased earnings under the options.

f. Changes in real (inflation-adjusted) income include increases in earnings for workers who would receive a higher wage, decreases in earnings for workers who would be jobless because of the minimum-wage increase, losses in income for business owners, decreases in income because of increases in prices, and increases in income generated by higher demand for goods and services.

g. Calculated using before-tax family cash income. Poverty thresholds vary with family size and composition. The definitions of income and of poverty thresholds are those used to determine the official poverty rate and are as defined by the Census Bureau. CBO projects that in 2016, the poverty threshold (in 2013 dollars) will be about $18,700 for a family of three and $24,100 for a family of four.

The increased earnings for low-wage workers resulting from the higher minimum wage would total $31 billion, by CBO's estimate.[2] However, those earnings would not go only to low-income families, because many low-wage workers are not members of low-income families. Just 19 percent of the $31 billion would accrue to families with earnings below the poverty threshold, whereas 29 percent would accrue to families earning more than three times the poverty threshold, CBO estimates.[3]

Moreover, the increased earnings for some workers would be accompanied by reductions in real (inflation-adjusted) income for the people who became jobless because of the minimum-wage increase, for business owners, and for consumers facing higher prices. CBO examined family

---

2. All effects on income are reported for the second half of 2016; annualized (that is, multiplied by two); and presented in 2013 dollars.

3. Poverty thresholds vary with family size and composition; CBO projects that in 2016, the poverty threshold (in 2013 dollars) will be about $18,700 for a family of three and $24,100 for a family of four.

income overall and for various income groups, reaching the following conclusions:

■ Once the increases and decreases in income for all workers are taken into account, overall real income would rise by $2 billion.

■ Real income would increase, on net, by $5 billion for families whose income will be below the poverty threshold under current law, boosting their average family income by about 3 percent and moving about 900,000 people, on net, above the poverty threshold (out of the roughly 45 million people who are projected to be below that threshold under current law).

■ Families whose income would have been between one and three times the poverty threshold would receive, on net, $12 billion in additional real income. About $2 billion, on net, would go to families whose income would have been between three and six times the poverty threshold.

■ Real income would decrease, on net, by $17 billion for families whose income would otherwise have been six times the poverty threshold or more, lowering their average family income by 0.4 percent.

Effects of the $9.00 Option on Employment and Income. The $9.00 option would reduce employment by about 100,000 workers, or by less than 0.1 percent, CBO projects. There is about a two-thirds chance that the effect would be in the range between a very slight increase in employment and a reduction in employment of 200,000 workers, in CBO's assessment. Roughly 7.6 million workers who will earn up to $9.00 per hour under current law would have higher earnings during an average week in the second half of 2016 if this option was implemented, CBO estimates, and some people earning more than $9.00 would have higher earnings as well.

The increased earnings for low-wage workers resulting from the higher minimum wage would total $9 billion; 22 percent of that sum would accrue to families with income below the poverty threshold, whereas 33 percent would accrue to families earning more than three times the poverty threshold, CBO estimates.

For family income overall and for various income groups, CBO estimates the following:

■ Once the increases and decreases in income for all workers are taken into account, overall real income would rise by $1 billion.

■ Real income would increase, on net, by about $1 billion for families whose income will be below the poverty threshold under current law, boosting their average family income by about 1 percent and moving about 300,000 people, on net, above the poverty threshold.

■ Families whose income would have been between one and three times the poverty threshold would receive, on net, $3 billion in additional real income. About $1 billion, on net, would go to families whose income would have been between three and six times the poverty threshold.

■ Real income would decrease, on net, by $4 billion for families whose income would otherwise have been six times the poverty threshold or more, lowering their average family income by about 0.1 percent.

Effects of a Minimum-Wage Increase on the Federal Budget. In addition to affecting employment and family income, increasing the federal minimum wage would affect the federal budget directly by increasing the wages that the federal government paid to a small number of hourly employees and indirectly by boosting the prices of some goods and services purchased by the government. Most of those costs would need to be covered by discretionary appropriations, which are capped through 2021 under current law.

Federal spending and taxes would also be indirectly affected by the increases in real income for some people and the reduction in real income for others. As a group, workers with increased earnings would pay more in taxes and receive less in federal benefits of certain types than they would have otherwise. However, people who became jobless because of the minimum-wage increase, business owners, and consumers facing higher prices would see a reduction in real income and would collectively pay less in taxes and receive more in federal benefits than they would have otherwise. CBO concludes that the net effect on the federal budget of raising the minimum wage would probably be a small decrease in budget deficits for several years but a small increase in budget deficits thereafter. It is unclear whether the effect for the coming decade as a whole would be a small increase or a small decrease in budget deficits.

The Current Federal Minimum Wage

The federal minimum wage was established by the Fair Labor Standards Act of 1938 (FLSA) and currently applies to about two-thirds of workers in the public and private sectors. Workers whose compensation depends heavily on tips (such as waiters and bartenders) are subject to a special arrangement: The regular minimum wage applies to their compensation including tips, and a lower cash minimum wage applies to their compensation excluding tips. The FLSA also has exceptions for workers and employers of certain types, including a provision permitting employers to pay teenage workers $4.25 per hour during their first 90 days of employment.[4]

The nominal federal minimum wage has risen over the years. The most recent changes, which took effect in July 2007, raised the minimum wage in three steps from $5.15 per hour (in nominal dollars) to $7.25 in July 2009, where it stands today.[5] However, the real value of the minimum wage has both risen and fallen, as the nominal increases have subsequently been eroded by inflation (see Figure 1).[6] That erosion was most pronounced between January 1981 and April 1990 and between September 1997 and July 2007—each a period of nearly 10 years during which the nominal value of the minimum wage was unchanged.

Many states and localities have minimum-wage laws that apply, along with federal law, to employers within their jurisdiction. In recent years, states and localities have been particularly active in boosting their minimum wage; as of January 2014, 21 states and the District of Columbia had a minimum wage that was higher than the federal one. In 11 of those states, the minimum wage is adjusted automatically each year with inflation, and in four more, plus the District of Columbia, future increases have

already been legislated. In California, for example, the minimum wage is scheduled to increase from $8.00 to $9.00 in July 2014 and to $10.00 in January 2016. Some localities also have minimum wages that are higher than the applicable state or federal minimum wage; in San Francisco, for instance, the minimum wage is $10.74 per hour. Another 20 states have minimum wages equal to the federal minimum wage (and linked to it, in some cases). In some of those states, the state laws apply to some workers and employers who are not covered by the FLSA. At the moment, about half of all workers in the United States live in states where the applicable minimum wage is more than $7.25 per hour. The applicable minimum wage in those states ranges from $7.40 to $9.32 per hour (see Figure 2).

Minimum-wage workers are sometimes thought of primarily as teenagers from nonpoor families who are working part time, but that is not the case now. Of the 5.5 million workers who earned within 25 cents of the minimum wage in 2013, three-quarters were at least 20 years old and two-fifths worked full time. Their median family income was about $30,000, CBO estimates. (Some of the family incomes within that group of workers were substantially higher or lower than that amount, in part because the number of working adults in their families varied.)

Two Options for Increasing the Federal Minimum Wage

Lawmakers have proposed various options for increasing the federal minimum wage, including several that would increase it to $10.10 per hour and subsequently index it

---

4. For details about the FLSA's minimum-wage requirements, see Fair Labor Standards Act of 1938, as amended, 29 U.S.C. §201 et seq. (2012). See also Department of Labor, "Minimum Wage and Overtime Pay" (accessed January 8, 2014), www.dol.gov/compliance/guide/minwage.htm.

5. After CBO completed its analysis of increasing the federal minimum wage, the President issued an executive order, entitled "Minimum Wage for Contractors," that established a minimum wage of $10.10 per hour for certain individuals working under new contracts with the federal government, beginning on January 1, 2015. That order slightly reduces the number of workers who would be affected by increasing the federal minimum wage and thus slightly reduces the estimated effects presented in this report.

6. Adjusted for inflation, the federal minimum wage reached its historical peak in 1968. In that year, its value in 1968 dollars was $1.60, which is equal to $8.41 in 2013 dollars if the conversion is done with the price index for personal consumption expenditures published by the Bureau of Economic Analysis. CBO generally uses that index when adjusting labor market data for inflation, considering it a more accurate measure than a common alternative—the consumer price index for all urban consumers (CPI-U), which is published by the Bureau of Labor Statistics (BLS). According to many analysts, the CPI-U overstates increases in the cost of living because it does not fully account for the fact that consumers generally adjust their spending patterns as some prices change relative to other prices and because of a statistical bias related to the limited amount of price data that BLS can collect. The value of $1.60 in 1968 dollars is equal to $10.71 in 2013 dollars if the conversion is done with the CPI-U.

Figure 1.

Workers' Hourly Wages and the Federal Minimum Wage, 1973 to 2018

(2013 dollars per hour)

Source: Congressional Budget Office based on monthly data from the Census Bureau's Current Population Survey and on data from the Department of Labor.

Note: CBO converted wages to 2013 dollars using the price index for personal consumption expenditures published by the Bureau of Economic Analysis. For example, nominal values in 2016 of $10.10 and $9.00 were adjusted downward to account for projected inflation between 2013 and 2016. After 2016, the minimum wage under the $10.10 option would increase slightly in the 2013 dollars shown in this figure because it would be indexed to the consumer price index, which would grow faster than the price index for personal consumption expenditures, CBO projects. Values for the federal minimum wage—both actual values and projected values under the $10.10 option, the $9.00 option, and current law—are as of July 1 of each year.

a.   The hourly wage of workers not paid hourly was estimated as their weekly earnings divided by their usual hours worked per week. Values after those for 2013 are projected under current law.

b.   The minimum wage would rise (in three steps, starting in 2014) to $10.10 by July 1, 2016, and then be indexed to inflation.

c.   The minimum wage would rise (in two steps, starting in 2015) to $9.00 by July 1, 2016, and would not be subsequently indexed to inflation.

for inflation.[7] CBO has assessed the impact of such an option, as well as the impact of a smaller increase that would boost the minimum wage to $9.00 per hour and would not link future increases to inflation. (See Appendix A for information about how CBO conducted its assessments.) The options that CBO analyzed would not change other provisions of the FLSA, such as the one that applies to wages for teenage workers during their first 90 days of employment.

A $10.10 Option
CBO examined an option that would increase the federal minimum wage from $7.25 per hour to $8.20 on July 1,

2014; to $9.15 one year after that; and to $10.10 after another year. The increase in the minimum wage between 2014 and 2016 under this option would be about 40 percent, roughly the same percentage as the total increase from 2007 to 2009 but larger than several earlier increases. Each year after that, the minimum wage would rise with the consumer price index.[8]

In addition, this option would raise the minimum cash wage for tipped workers from $2.13 per hour to $4.90 in three steps timed to coincide with the changes in the minimum wage. Then, starting in 2017, the minimum

---

7.   See, for example, S. 460, the Fair Minimum Wage Act of 2013; S. 1737, the Minimum Wage Fairness Act; and H.R. 3939, the Invest in United States Act of 2014. Another proposal (H.R. 3746, the Fair Minimum Wage Act of 2013) would increase the minimum wage to $11.00 and subsequently index it for inflation.

8.   The $10.10 option is based on the provisions of S. 460, the Fair Minimum Wage Act of 2013. (The FLSA and S. 460 also apply to Puerto Rico and certain other U.S. territories, but because of limitations in available data, CBO's analysis is limited to the effects of minimum-wage increases on employment and family income in the 50 states and the District of Columbia.)

Figure 2.

Shares of All Workers, by States' Applicable Minimum Wage, 2014

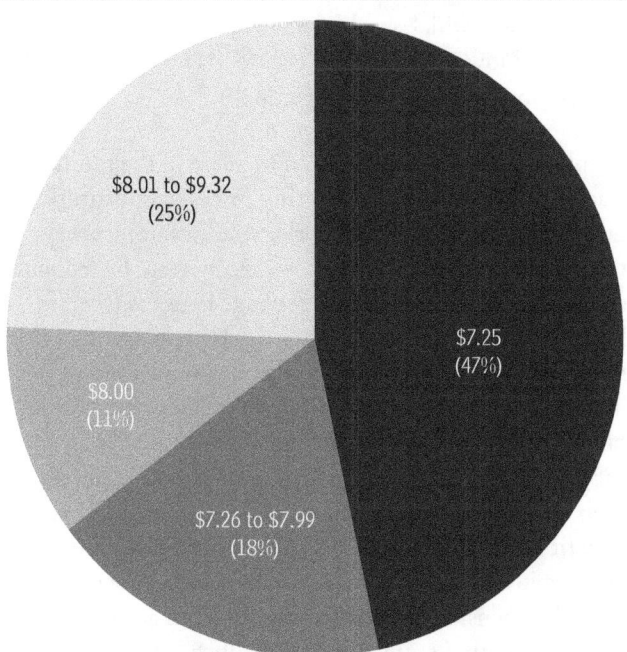

Source: Congressional Budget Office based on monthly data from the Census Bureau's Current Population Survey and on data from the Department of Labor.

Note: As of January 1, 2014, 21 states and the District of Columbia had a minimum wage above the federal minimum wage. The highest was $9.32 in the state of Washington.

cash wage for tipped workers would rise by 95 cents each year until it reached 70 percent of the minimum wage (which would occur in 2019, by CBO's estimate); in subsequent years, it would be tied to inflation.

A $9.00 Option

CBO also examined a smaller change that would increase the federal minimum wage from $7.25 per hour to $8.10 on July 1, 2015, and to $9.00 on July 1, 2016. The minimum cash wage for tipped workers would increase when the minimum wage increased, and by the same percentage. The increase in the minimum wage would start one year later than it would under the $10.10 option. Like previous minimum-wage increases, this one would not be indexed to subsequent inflation. This $9.00 option is more similar than the $10.10 option to minimum-wage increases studied in the economics literature in a number of respects: the size of the increase, the portion of the workforce that it would affect, and the fact that its real value would be eroded over time.

How Increases in the Minimum Wage Affect Employment and Family Income

In general, increases in the minimum wage probably reduce employment for some low-wage workers. At the same time, however, they increase family income for many more low-wage workers.

Employment

According to conventional economic analysis, increasing the minimum wage reduces employment in two ways. First, higher wages increase the cost to employers of producing goods and services. The employers pass some of those increased costs on to consumers in the form of higher prices, and those higher prices, in turn, lead the consumers to purchase fewer of the goods and services. The employers consequently produce fewer goods and services, so they hire fewer workers. That is known as a scale effect, and it reduces employment among both low-wage workers and higher-wage workers.

Second, a minimum-wage increase raises the cost of low-wage workers relative to other inputs that employers use to produce goods and services, such as machines, technology, and more productive higher-wage workers. Some employers respond by reducing their use of low-wage workers and shifting toward those other inputs. That is known as a substitution effect, and it reduces employment among low-wage workers but increases it among higher-wage workers.

However, conventional economic analysis might not apply in certain circumstances. For example, when a firm is hiring more workers and needs to boost pay for existing workers doing the same work—to match what it needs to pay to recruit the new workers—hiring a new worker costs the company not only that new worker's wages but also the additional wages paid to retain other workers. Under those circumstances, which arise more often when finding a new job is time-consuming and costly for workers, increasing the minimum wage means that businesses have to pay the existing workers more, whether or not a new employee was hired; as a result, it lowers the additional cost of hiring a new employee, leading to increased employment. There is a wide range of views among economists about the merits of the conventional analysis and of this alternative.

The low-wage workers whose wages are affected by increases in the minimum wage include not only those workers who would otherwise have earned less than the minimum but also, in some cases, workers who would have earned slightly more than the minimum. After a minimum-wage increase, some employers try to preserve differentials in pay that existed before—for example, so that supervisors continue to be paid more than the people they supervise—by raising the wages of people who previously earned a little more than the new minimum. Also, some wages determined by collective bargaining agreements are tied to the federal minimum wage and could therefore increase. As a result, an increase in the minimum wage causes some workers who would otherwise have earned slightly more than the new minimum wage to become jobless, for the same reasons that lower-wage workers do; at the same time, some firms hire more of those workers as substitutes for the workers whose wages were required to be increased.

The change in employment of low-wage workers caused by a minimum-wage increase differs substantially from firm to firm. Employment falls more at firms whose customers are very sensitive to price increases, because demand for their products or services declines more as prices rise, so those firms cut production more than other firms do. Employment also falls more at firms that can readily substitute other inputs for low-wage workers and at firms where low-wage workers constitute a large fraction of input costs. However, when low-wage workers have fewer employment alternatives overall, employment can fall less at firms that offset some of the increased costs with higher productivity from employees' working harder to keep their better-paying jobs and with the lower cost of filling vacant positions that results from higher wages' attracting more applicants and reducing turnover. Some firms, particularly those that do not employ many low-wage workers but that compete with firms that do, might see demand rise for their goods and services as their competitors' costs rise; such firms would tend to hire more low-wage workers as a result.

The change in employment of low-wage workers also differs over time. At first, when the minimum wage rises, some firms employ fewer low-wage workers, while other firms do not; the reduced employment is concentrated in businesses and industries where higher prices result in larger reductions in demand. Over a longer time frame, however, more firms replace low-wage workers with inputs that are relatively less expensive, such as more productive higher-wage workers. Thus, the percentage reduction in employment of low-wage workers is generally greater in the long term than in the short term, in

CBO's assessment. (However, the total reduction in employment might be smaller in the long term; that total depends not only on the percentage reduction in employment of low-wage workers but also on the number of such workers, which could decline over time if wage growth for low-wage workers exceeded any increase in the minimum wage, all else being equal.)

Employers might respond to an increase in the minimum wage in ways other than boosting prices or substituting other inputs for low-wage workers. For example, they might partly offset a minimum-wage increase by reducing other costs, including workers' fringe benefits (such as health insurance or pensions) and job perks (such as free meals). As a result, a higher minimum wage might increase total compensation (which includes benefits and perks) less than it increased cash wages alone. That, in turn, would give employers a smaller incentive to reduce their employment of low-wage workers. However, such benefit reductions would probably be modest, in part because low-wage workers generally receive few benefits related to pensions or health insurance. In addition, tax rules specify that employers who reduce low-wage workers' nonwage benefits can face unfavorable tax treatment for higher-wage workers' nonwage benefits. Employers can also partly offset higher wages for low-wage workers by reducing either formal training or informal mentoring and coaching. The evidence on how much employers reduce benefits, training, or other costs is mixed. (For examples of such evidence, see Appendix B.)

An increase in the minimum wage also affects the employment of low-wage workers in the short term through changes in the economywide demand for goods and services. A higher minimum wage shifts income from higher-wage consumers and business owners to low-wage workers. Because those low-wage workers tend to spend a larger fraction of their earnings, some firms see increased demand for their goods and services, boosting the employment of low-wage workers and higher-wage workers alike. That effect is larger when the economy is weaker, and it is larger in regions of the country where the economy is weaker.

Low-wage workers are not the only ones whose employment can be affected by a minimum-wage increase; the employment of higher-wage workers can be affected as well, in several ways. Firms that cut back on production tend to reduce the number of both higher-wage workers and low-wage workers. But once a minimum-wage increase makes higher-wage workers relatively less expensive, firms sometimes hire more of them to replace a larger number of less productive low-wage workers. Another factor affecting higher-wage workers is the increase in the economywide demand for goods and services. All in all, a higher minimum wage tends to increase the employment of higher-wage workers slightly, according to CBO's analysis.

Family Income

For most families with low-wage workers, a higher minimum wage boosts family income, because of the increase in earnings that many of those workers (including those whose wages were slightly above the new minimum) receive. A much smaller number of low-wage workers become jobless and therefore experience a decline in earnings because of the higher minimum wage.

For families with low-wage workers, the effect of a higher minimum wage depends on how many such workers are in a family, whether those workers become jobless (and, if so, for how long), and whether there are other changes in family income. For instance, the decline in income from losing a job can be offset in part by increases in nonlabor income, such as unemployment compensation, or by increases in the work of other family members.

For business owners, family income (including income for shareholders) falls to the extent that firms' profits are reduced. In addition, real family income for many people tends to fall a bit, because the increase in prices of goods and services reduces families' purchasing power.

The effects on total national income of an increase in the minimum wage differ in the long term and in the short term. In the long term, the key determinant of the nation's output and income is the size and quality of the workforce, the stock of productive capital (such as factories and computers), and the efficiency with which workers and capital are used to produce goods and services (known as total factor productivity). Raising the minimum wage probably reduces employment, in CBO's assessment. In the long term, that reduction in the workforce lowers the nation's output and income a little, which means that the income losses of some people are slightly larger than the income gains of others. In the short term, by contrast, the nation's output and income can deviate from the amounts that would typically arise from a given workforce, capital stock, and productivity in response to changes in the economywide demand for

goods and services. Raising the minimum wage increases that demand, in CBO's assessment, because the families that experience increases in income tend to raise their consumption more than the families that experience decreases in income tend to reduce their consumption. In the short term, that increase in demand raises the nation's output and income slightly, which means that the income losses of some people are slightly smaller than the income gains of others.

CBO's Findings About Employment and Family Income

CBO estimated the effects on employment and family income of both the $10.10 option and the $9.00 option for raising the federal minimum wage.[9] CBO's estimates are for the second half of 2016 because that would be the point at which the minimum wage reached $10.10 under the first option and $9.00 under the second. In either case, the increase in the minimum wage would have two principal effects on low-wage workers: The large majority would have higher wages and family income, but a much smaller group would be jobless and have much lower family income. Once the other changes in income were taken into account, families whose income would be below six times the poverty threshold under current law would see a small increase in income, on net, and families whose income would be higher under current law would see reductions in income, on net. In addition, in either case, higher-wage workers would see a small increase in the number of jobs.

Increases in the minimum wage would raise the wages not only for many workers who would otherwise have earned less than the new minimum but also for some workers who would otherwise have earned slightly more than the new minimum, as discussed above. CBO's analysis focused on workers who are projected to earn less than $11.50 per hour in 2016 under current law (who, in this report, are generally referred to as low-wage workers). People with certain characteristics are more likely to be in that group and are therefore more likely to be affected by increases in the minimum wage like those that CBO examined. For example, in 2016, 88 percent of the

---

9. For an estimate of the effect on employment of a previous proposal to increase the minimum wage, see Congressional Budget Office, private-sector mandate statement for S. 277, the Fair Minimum Wage Act of 2001 (May 9, 2001), www.cbo.gov/publication/13043.

people earning such wages will be at least 20 years old, 56 percent will be female, and 91 percent will not have attained a bachelor's degree, CBO estimates (see Table 2).

Effects of the Options on Employment

According to CBO's central estimate, implementing the $10.10 option would reduce employment by roughly 500,000 workers in the second half of 2016, relative to what would happen under current law.[10] That decrease would be the net result of two effects: a slightly larger decrease in jobs for low-wage workers (because of their higher cost) and an increase of a few tens of thousands of jobs for other workers (because of greater demand for goods and services).[11] By CBO's estimate, about 1½ percent of the 33 million workers who otherwise would have earned less than $11.50 per hour would be jobless— either because they lost a job or because they could not find a job—as a result of the increase in the minimum wage.

Those job losses among low-wage workers would be concentrated among people who are projected to earn less than $10.10 an hour under current law. Some workers who would otherwise have earned between $10.10 and $11.50 per hour would also see an increase in their wages, which would tend to reduce their employment as well, CBO estimates. However, some firms might hire more of those workers as substitutes for the lower-paid workers whose wages had been increased. Those two factors would probably be roughly offsetting, CBO anticipates, so the number of such workers who were employed would probably not change significantly.

The overall reduction in employment could be smaller or larger than CBO's central estimate. In CBO's assessment, there is about a two-thirds chance that the effect of the $10.10 option would be in the range between a very slight decrease in employment and a decrease of

1.0 million workers; thus, there is a one-third chance that the effect would be either above or below that range. The most important factors contributing to the width of the range are uncertainty about the growth of wages over the next three years (which influences the number of workers who would be affected by the minimum-wage increase, as well as the extent to which the increase would raise their wages) and uncertainty about the responsiveness of employment to an increase in wages. For example, if wage growth under current law was slower than CBO projects, implementing the increase would result in more people with increased wages and a greater reduction in employment than CBO's central estimate suggests.

Under the $9.00 option, employment would decline by about 100,000 workers in the second half of 2016, relative to what it would be under current law, according to CBO's central estimate. That estimate is much smaller than the central estimate for the $10.10 option for three reasons: Fewer workers would be affected; the change in their wages would be smaller; and four aspects of the $9.00 option would make employment in 2016 less responsive to a minimum-wage increase, CBO expects.[12] The first of those four aspects is that the $9.00 option is not indexed to inflation, so some employers would probably refrain from reducing employment, knowing that inflation would erode the cost of paying higher wages. Second, under the $9.00 option, the second half of 2016 arrives one year after the initial increase in the minimum wage—rather than two years, as under the $10.10 option—and employers would be less likely to reduce employment soon after an increase in the minimum wage than they would be over a longer period. Third, because the cost of paying higher wages under the $9.00 option is smaller than that of the $10.10 option, CBO expects that fewer employers would find it desirable to incur the adjustment costs of reducing employment (such as installation of new equipment). Fourth, the $9.00 option would apply to a smaller share of the workforce. Four percent of the labor hours in the economy will be worked

---

10. A central estimate is one that uses values at or near the midpoints of estimated ranges for key inputs.

11. In this report, phrases referring to changes in the number of jobs are used interchangeably with phrases referring to changes in employment. Technically, however, if a low-wage worker holds multiple jobs and loses one of them, that would represent a reduction of one job but no change in employment (because the worker would remain employed). About 5 percent of low-wage workers will hold more than one job under current law, CBO projects. Therefore, for any given reduction in employment, the reduction in the number of jobs will be slightly larger.

12. Under the $9.00 option, the central estimate of the responsiveness of employment to a change in the applicable minimum wage is -0.075 for teenagers, for example, which means that the employment of teenagers would be reduced by three-quarters of one percent after a 10 percent change in the minimum wage. The equivalent estimate under the $10.10 option is -0.10. See Appendix A for more information.

Table 2.

Projected Characteristics of Low-Wage Workers, Second Half of 2016

Characteristic	Percentage of All Workers With Characteristic Who Will Be Low-Wage	Percentage of Low-Wage Workers With Characteristic
Age		
16 to 19	87	12
20 and older	22	88
All	24	100
Sex		
Female	28	56
Male	21	44
All	24	100
Educational Attainment		
Less than high school	58	21
High school graduate or some college	30	70
Bachelor's degree	7	10
All	24	100
Hours Worked per Week		
Fewer than 35	58	47
35 or more	16	53
All	24	100
Number of Employees in Firm		
Fewer than 50	30	48
50 or more	19	52
All	24	100

Source: Congressional Budget Office based on monthly and annual data from the Census Bureau's Current Population Survey.

Note: Low-wage workers are people who are projected, under current law in the second half of 2016, to be paid less than $11.50 per hour.

by people who will earn up to $9.00 per hour under current law and who would either receive a wage increase or be jobless if the $9.00 option was implemented, CBO estimates. In contrast, about 10 percent of labor hours will be worked by people who will earn up to $10.10 per hour under current law and who would either receive a wage increase or be jobless if the $10.10 option was implemented. Thus, the $9.00 option would cause a correspondingly smaller increase in costs, which employers would be likely to absorb less through reductions in employment and more in other ways.

In CBO's assessment, there is a two-thirds chance that the effect of the $9.00 option would be in the range between a very slight increase in the number of jobs and a loss of 200,000 jobs.[13] If employment increased under either option, in CBO's judgment, it would probably be because increased demand for goods and services (resulting from the shift of income from higher-income to

lower-income people) had boosted economic activity and generated more jobs than were lost as a direct result of the increase in the cost of hiring low-wage workers.

CBO has not analyzed the effects of either option on the number of hours worked by people who would remain employed or on the decision to search actively for work and join the labor force by people who would not

---

13. In a recent survey, leading economists were asked whether they agreed with the statement that "raising the federal minimum wage to $9 per hour would make it noticeably harder for low-skilled workers to find employment." When the results were weighted by the respondents' confidence, 40 percent of the economists agreed with the statement, 38 percent disagreed, and 22 percent were uncertain. However, the survey did not specify how large a drop in employment was meant by "noticeably harder . . . to find employment." See University of Chicago Booth School of Business, "Minimum Wage" (published February 26, 2013; accessed January 8, 2014), http://tinyurl.com/aa52pfo.

otherwise be working. Therefore, the agency has not reported the effects of the options on full-time-equivalent employment or on the unemployment rate.

Effects of the Options on Family Income

Among the 33 million low-wage workers earning less than $11.50 per hour in the second half of 2016 under current law, CBO estimates, real earnings would increase by $31 billion as a result of higher wages if the $10.10 option was implemented. (All amounts of income reported for that period are annualized—that is, multiplied by two—and reported in 2013 dollars.) About 16.5 million workers who will earn less than $10.10 per hour under current law would receive higher wages, CBO estimates, and some workers who will earn between $10.10 and $11.50 per hour under current law would receive higher wages as well.[14] Most of the additional income would accrue to families with fairly low income, but a substantial portion would also be received by low-wage workers in higher-income families—29 percent and 6 percent by families who would otherwise have had income greater than three and six times the federal poverty threshold, respectively.

That increase in income resulting from higher wages would be accompanied by reductions of a similar amount in real income from several other sources: decreases in earnings for workers who would be jobless because of the minimum-wage increase; losses in income for business owners; and increases in prices of goods and services, which would reduce people's purchasing power. In addition, a few higher-wage workers would be employed and earn more because of increased demand for goods and services resulting from the minimum-wage increase.

Once all those factors are taken into account, CBO estimates that the net changes in real income would be an increase of about $5 billion for families whose income would have been below the poverty threshold under current law; an increase of $12 billion for families whose income would have been between one and three times the poverty threshold; an increase of $2 billion for families whose income would have been between three and six times the poverty threshold; and a *decrease* of $17 billion for families whose income would have been greater than

that (see Figure 3). (In 2016, six times the poverty threshold will be roughly $120,000 for a family of three and $150,000 for a family of four, CBO projects.) According to CBO's estimates, the increase in earnings for the few low-wage workers living in that last group of families would be more than offset by income reductions, in part because the losses in business income and in real income from price increases would be concentrated in those families (see Table 3).

Families whose income will be below the poverty threshold in 2016 under current law will have an average income of $10,700, CBO projects (see Table 4 on page 14). The agency estimates that the $10.10 option would raise their average real income by about $300, or 2.8 percent. For families whose income would otherwise have been between the poverty threshold and 1.5 times that amount, average real income would increase by about $300, or 1.1 percent. The increase in average income would be smaller, both in dollar amounts and as a share of family income, for families whose income would have been between 1.5 times and six times the poverty threshold. And for families whose income would otherwise have been greater than six times the poverty threshold, the total effect of the $10.10 option would be a reduction in average real income of about $700, or 0.4 percent. But the effects of a minimum-wage increase on family income would vary even among families with similar incomes under current law. For example, many families with income less than six times the poverty threshold would see their income rise; but income for a smaller set of those families would decline, because some low-wage workers would lose jobs that they would otherwise have.

Under current law, CBO projects, there will be roughly 45 million people in families whose income is below the poverty threshold in 2016. The $10.10 option would reduce that number by about 900,000, or 2 percent, according to CBO's estimate. That estimate takes into account both families whose income would increase and move them out of poverty and families whose income would fall and move them into poverty. The estimate uses a measure of family income called cash income, which is used to determine the official poverty rate. Cash income includes earnings and cash transfers from the government, such as Supplemental Security Income benefits. It excludes noncash transfers, such as benefits from Medicaid and the Supplemental Nutrition Assistance Program (SNAP, formerly known as the Food Stamp program); taxes; and tax credits, such as the earned

---

14. CBO did not estimate the number of workers in the latter group who would receive higher wages as a result of the increase in the minimum wage; instead, it applied an estimated average percentage increase in wages to all workers in that group. See Appendix A for more information.

Figure 3.

Estimated Effects on Real Family Income of an Increase in the Federal Minimum Wage, Second Half of 2016

(Billions of 2013 dollars, annualized)

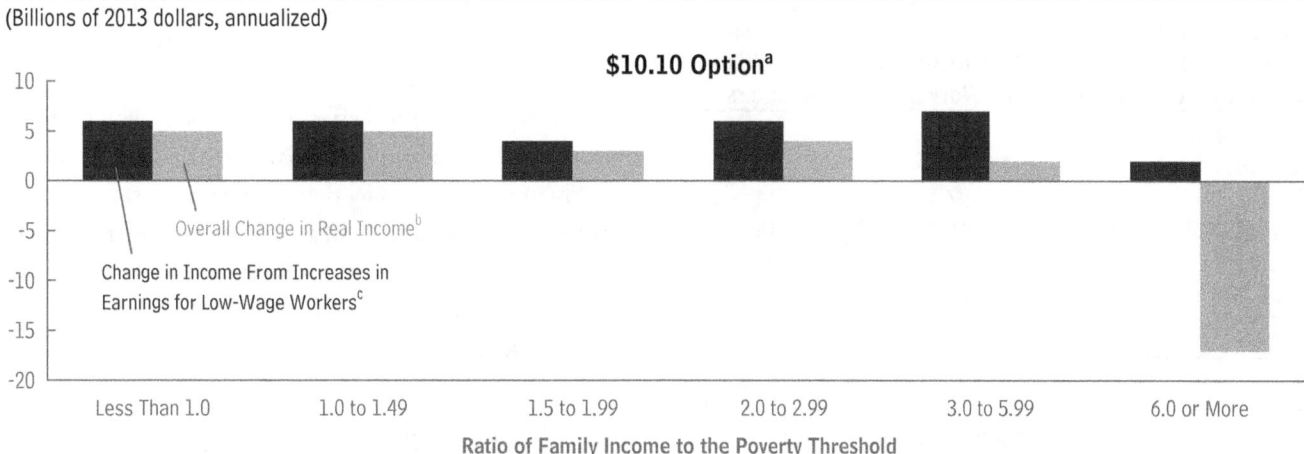

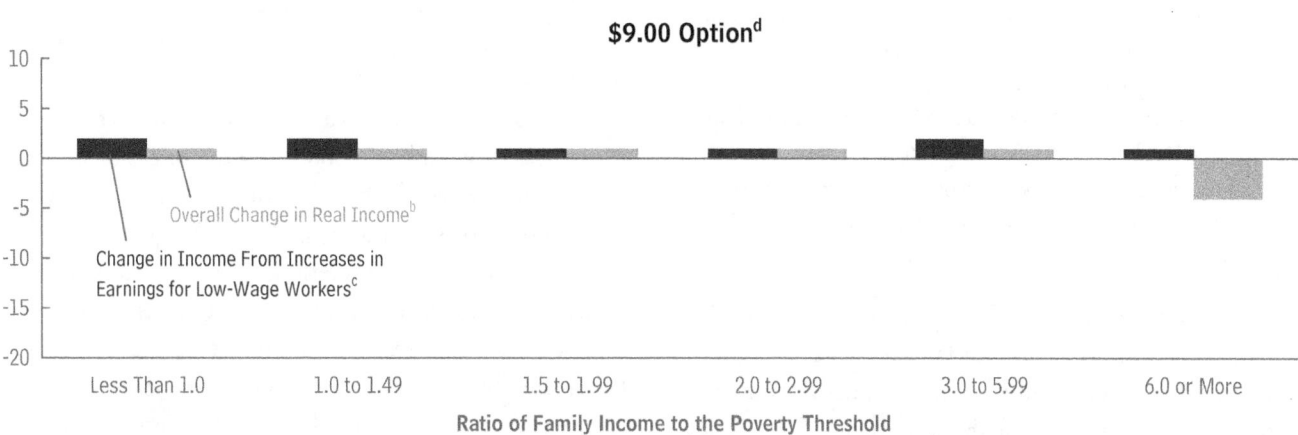

Source: Congressional Budget Office based on annual data from the Census Bureau's Current Population Survey.

Note: Calculated using before-tax family cash income. Poverty thresholds vary with family size and composition. The definitions of income and of poverty thresholds are those used to determine the official poverty rate and are as defined by the Census Bureau. CBO projects that in 2016, the poverty threshold (in 2013 dollars) will be about $18,700 for a family of three and $24,100 for a family of four.

a.   The minimum wage would rise (in three steps, starting in 2014) to $10.10 by July 1, 2016, and then be indexed to inflation.

b.   Changes in real (inflation-adjusted) income include increases in earnings for workers who would receive a higher wage, decreases in earnings for workers who would be jobless because of the minimum-wage increase, losses in income for business owners, decreases in income because of increases in prices, and increases in income generated by higher demand for goods and services.

c.   Increases in earnings for workers who are projected, under current law, to be paid less than $11.50 per hour.

d.   The minimum wage would rise (in two steps, starting in 2015) to $9.00 by July 1, 2016, and would not be subsequently indexed to inflation.

income tax credit (EITC). (Because the EITC provides cash to many lower-income families, it is sometimes compared with the federal minimum wage in discussions about how to boost lower-income families' resources; see Box 1 on page 15.)

Implementing the $9.00 option would have a smaller effect on family income and on the number of people in

poverty than implementing the $10.10 option would. About 7.6 million workers who will earn less than $9.00 per hour under current law would receive higher wages, CBO estimates, and so would some workers who will earn more than $9.00 per hour under current law. Once all factors are taken into account, CBO estimates that the net changes in total real income would be an increase of about $1 billion for families whose income

Table 3.

Projected Shares of Workers, by Family Income Group, Second Half of 2016

Ratio of Family Income to the Poverty Threshold	Percentage of All Workers	Percentage of Low-Wage Workers[a]
Less Than 1.0	6	20
1.0 to 1.49	6	16
1.5 to 1.99	7	14
2.0 to 2.99	16	18
3.0 to 5.99	39	24
6.0 or More	26	9
Total	100	100

Source: Congressional Budget Office based on annual data from the Census Bureau's Current Population Survey.

Note: Calculated using before-tax family cash income. Poverty thresholds vary with family size and composition. The definitions of income and of poverty thresholds are those used to determine the official poverty rate and are as defined by the Census Bureau. CBO projects that in 2016, the poverty threshold (in 2013 dollars) will be about $18,700 for a family of three and $24,100 for a family of four.

a. Low-wage workers are people who are projected, under current law in the second half of 2016, to be paid less than $11.50 per hour.

would otherwise have been below the poverty threshold; increases totaling $4 billion for families whose income would have been between one and six times the poverty threshold; and a decrease of about $4 billion for families with higher income, as the declines in income for business owners and the loss of purchasing power would more than offset the increases in earnings for low-wage workers in that group. The agency estimates that average real family income would increase by about $100, or 0.9 percent, for families whose income would have been below the poverty threshold, and that the number of people living in such families would decline by about 300,000, or two-thirds of one percent. That is one-third of the decline in the number of people in poverty that would occur under the $10.10 option, CBO projects. For families whose income would otherwise have been six times the poverty threshold or more, average real family income would be lower by 0.1 percent.

The effects of the two options on average family income and on the number of people living in poverty are difficult to project accurately. Those effects depend on many things, including the extent to which the higher minimum wage would reduce employment, the length of time that people are not working, and the rate at which wages will grow over time under current law. The larger the reduction in employment for a given increase in the minimum wage, the less effective the policy would be at raising families out of poverty. And if wages grew more quickly under current law than CBO projects, fewer workers would have their wages increased under the options, and the effect on poverty would be smaller. (If those wages grew less quickly than CBO projects, the effect would be larger.)

The Effect of an Increase in the Minimum Wage on the Federal Budget

An increase in the federal minimum wage would directly affect the federal budget by requiring the government to increase wages for a small number of hourly federal employees. A minimum-wage increase would also indirectly affect the budget by boosting the prices of some goods and services purchased by the government. Most of those added costs for wages, goods, and services would need to be covered by discretionary appropriations, which are capped through 2021 under current law. If the caps were not adjusted, federal budget deficits would not be affected by the higher costs, but the benefits and government services that could be provided under the existing caps would be reduced. If, instead, lawmakers adjusted the caps to cover the higher costs, and if future appropriations equaled those higher caps, then deficits would be larger.

In addition, an increase in the federal minimum wage would indirectly affect the federal budget by changing people's income—raising real income for some workers while reducing the real income of people who would be jobless because of the minimum-wage increase, of business owners, and of consumers facing higher prices. As a group, the workers receiving an earnings increase would pay more in taxes and receive less in benefits than they would have otherwise, reducing the federal budget deficit; however, the workers, business owners, and consumers with reduced income would pay less in taxes and receive more in benefits, increasing the deficit.

Table 4.

Estimated Effects on Average Real Family Income of an Increase in the Federal Minimum Wage, Second Half of 2016

Ratio of Family Income to the Poverty Threshold	Average Real Family Income Before the Wage Change (2013 dollars, annualized)	Change in Average Real Family Income	
		2013 Dollars, Annualized	Percent
$10.10 Option[a]			
Less Than 1.0	10,700	300	2.8
1.0 to 1.49	26,300	300	1.1
1.5 to 1.99	36,300	200	0.6
2.0 to 2.99	51,400	200	0.4
3.0 to 5.99	86,600	*	**
6.0 or More	182,200	-700	-0.4
$9.00 Option[b]			
Less Than 1.0	10,700	100	0.9
1.0 to 1.49	26,300	100	0.4
1.5 to 1.99	36,300	100	0.3
2.0 to 2.99	51,400	100	0.2
3.0 to 5.99	86,600	*	**
6.0 or More	182,200	-200	-0.1

Source: Congressional Budget Office based on annual data from the Census Bureau's Current Population Survey.

Notes: Changes in real (inflation-adjusted) income include increases in earnings for workers who would receive a higher wage, decreases in earnings for workers who would be jobless because of the minimum-wage increase, losses in income for business owners, decreases in income because of increases in prices, and increases in income generated by higher demand for goods and services. Results are weighted by the number of people in the family; for example, when CBO calculated the averages, a family of three would be represented three times.

Calculated using before-tax family cash income. Poverty thresholds vary with family size and composition. The definitions of income and of poverty thresholds are those used to determine the official poverty rate and are as defined by the Census Bureau. CBO projects that in 2016, the poverty threshold (in 2013 dollars) will be about $18,700 for a family of three and $24,100 for a family of four.

* = between zero and $50; ** = between zero and 0.05 percent.

a.   The minimum wage would rise (in three steps, starting in 2014) to $10.10 by July 1, 2016, and then be indexed to inflation.

b.   The minimum wage would rise (in two steps, starting in 2015) to $9.00 by July 1, 2016, and would not be subsequently indexed to inflation.

CBO anticipates that the increases in income would be larger than the decreases in income for a few years after an increase in the minimum wage but would be smaller thereafter, as discussed earlier in the report. Further, for reasons discussed below, CBO anticipates that the effective marginal tax rate—that is, the combination of increased taxes and decreased benefits for each additional dollar of income—for the increases in income would probably be slightly larger than the effective marginal tax rate for the decreases in income. Combining those factors, CBO concludes that the net effect on the federal budget of raising the minimum wage would probably be a small decrease in budget deficits for several years but a small increase in budget deficits thereafter. It is unclear whether the effect for the coming decade as a whole would be a small increase or a small decrease in budget deficits.[15]

---

15. Cost estimates produced by CBO and the staff of the Joint Committee on Taxation (JCT) typically reflect the convention that macroeconomic variables, such as nominal output and the average price level, remain fixed at the values that they are projected to reach under current law. That is a long-standing convention—one that has been followed in the Congressional budget process since it was established in 1974 and by JCT since the early 1960s. Therefore, in producing a cost estimate for legislation that would increase the minimum wage, CBO and JCT would not incorporate some of the effects that such an increase would probably have on the economy. CBO was not able to assess how that approach might affect the estimated budgetary impact of increasing the minimum wage.

Box 1.

The Minimum Wage and the Earned Income Tax Credit

The earned income tax credit (EITC) provides cash assistance through the federal income tax system to low- and moderate-income families on the basis of their earnings, adjusted gross income, and family structure.[1] At first, as family earnings rise above zero (the "phase-in" range), EITC benefits increase; when earnings reach a certain point, the benefits stop increasing; when earnings reach a higher point (the beginning of the "phase-out" range), the benefits decline; and when earnings are high enough, the benefits end.[2] The maximum credit in 2014 is $5,460 for people with two qualifying children, for example. In 2016, the Congressional Budget Office (CBO) projects, the earnings level at which EITC benefits end will range from $15,100 for an unmarried worker without children to $54,300 for a married couple with three or more children.

Using the Minimum Wage or the EITC to Boost the Resources of Low-Income Families

To achieve any given increase in the resources of lower-income families would require a greater shift of resources in the economy if done by increasing the minimum wage than if done by increasing the EITC.[3] The reason is that a minimum-wage increase would add to the resources of most families of low-wage workers regardless of those families' income; for example, one-third of low-wage workers would be in families whose income was more than three times the federal poverty

threshold in 2016, and many of those workers would see their earnings rise if the minimum wage rose. By contrast, an increase in the EITC would go almost entirely to lower-income families.

The Interaction of the Minimum Wage and the EITC

An increase in the minimum wage would affect EITC benefits in different ways for different families. Many families whose income was initially within the phase-in range of the EITC schedule would find that increased earnings led to additional EITC benefits. But families whose income was initially in the phaseout range of the schedule would find that income gains from a higher minimum wage were partly offset by a reduction in EITC benefits. And families whose income was initially between the phase-in and phaseout ranges (a range in which EITC benefits do not change as earnings rise) and remained in that range after the minimum-wage increase would see no change in their EITC benefits. As for higher-income families with low-wage workers, they would not have been eligible for the EITC in the first place.

The EITC encourages more people in low-income families to work—particularly unmarried custodial parents, often mothers, for whom the EITC is larger than it is for people without children.[4] That increase in the number of available workers tends to reduce workers' wages, allowing some of the benefit of the EITC to accrue to employers, rather than to the workers themselves.[5] An increase in the minimum wage would shift some of that benefit from employers to workers by requiring the former to pay the latter more.

---

1. Adjusted gross income is income from all sources not specifically excluded from the tax code, minus certain deductions.

2. For a more extensive description of the EITC, see Congressional Budget Office, *Refundable Tax Credits* (January 2013), www.cbo.gov/publication/43767.

3. In a 2007 analysis, CBO compared the cost to employers of a change in the minimum wage that increased the income of poor families by a given amount to the cost to the federal government of a change in the EITC that increased the income of poor families by roughly the same amount. The cost to employers of the change in the minimum wage was much larger than the cost to the federal government of the change in the EITC. See Congressional Budget Office, *Response to a Request by Senator Grassley About the Effects of Increasing the Federal Minimum Wage Versus Expanding the Earned Income Tax Credit* (attachment to a letter to the Honorable Charles E. Grassley, January 9, 2007), www.cbo.gov/publication/18281. Most of the budgetary effect of an increase in the EITC shows up as an increase in spending, rather than as a reduction in revenues, because the credit is refundable and most of the total benefits represent amounts that are paid out rather than amounts that are used to offset other tax liabilities.

4. See Bruce D. Meyer and Dan T. Rosenbaum. "Welfare, the Earned Income Tax Credit, and the Labor Supply of Single Mothers," *Quarterly Journal of Economics*, vol. 116, no. 3 (August 2001), pp. 1063–1114, http://www.jstor.org/stable/2696426; and Nada Eissa and Jeffrey B. Liebman, "Labor Supply Response to the Earned Income Tax Credit," *Quarterly Journal of Economics*, vol. 111, no. 2 (May 1996), pp. 605–637, http://www.jstor.org/stable/2946689.

5. See David Lee and Emmanuel Saez, "Optimal Minimum Wage Policy in Competitive Labor Markets," *Journal of Public Economics*, vol. 96, no. 9 (October 2012), pp. 739–749, http://dx.doi.org/10.1016/j.jpubeco.2012.06.001; and Jesse Rothstein, "Is the EITC as Good as an NIT? Conditional Cash Transfers and Tax Incidence," *American Economic Journal: Economic Policy*, vol. 2, no. 1 (February 2010), pp. 177–208, http://www.jstor.org/stable/25760056.

Effects for People Whose Income Would Rise

As a group, the workers whose income rose because of a minimum-wage increase would consequently pay more in taxes and receive less in benefits.[16] CBO has previously estimated that the effective federal marginal tax rate on earnings for low- and moderate-income workers is 32 percent, on average; that is, the combination of increased taxes and decreased benefits equals, on average, about one-third of such a worker's added earnings.[17] CBO expects that workers receiving an increase in earnings from a boost to the minimum wage would face a similar rate, on average. Therefore, CBO expects that the reduction in the deficit associated with people whose earnings would rise would be about 32 percent of the increase in earnings for those workers.

Part of that deficit reduction would result from increased tax payments for the workers who were earning more. The largest part of that increase would consist of payroll taxes assessed for Social Security and Medicare, which are paid at a combined rate of 15.3 percent by most employees and employers.[18] The increase in earnings for some workers would also increase the amount that they owed in income taxes before refundable tax credits were taken

into account, although almost all of them would owe no tax or be in one of the two lowest federal income tax brackets. In addition, benefits from the EITC would fall for workers whose annual income was in the range where the credits decrease with income (see Box 1). (However, those benefits would rise for workers whose annual income remained in the income range where the credits increase with income, and some workers with increased earnings would qualify for a larger child tax credit.)

The rest of the deficit reduction would result from less federal spending (aside from the effects on refundable earned income and child tax credits) for the workers receiving an increase in earnings. Spending on cash and near-cash transfer programs (such as SNAP and Supplemental Security Income) would decline for those workers, because the amount of those benefits generally falls as income rises.[19] In addition, spending for premium assistance tax credits and cost-sharing subsidies for health insurance purchased through exchanges would decline for people who will be receiving such support under current law, because the amount of that support also generally falls as income rises.[20]

The estimated effective federal marginal tax rate of 32 percent does not include the budgetary effects of some people's moving out of Medicaid coverage or into subsidized insurance coverage through exchanges because their earnings had increased.[21] Some of those effects would raise federal costs and others would lower them. In particular, some people who will be eligible for Medicaid

---

16. In the short term, some people would also see an increase in income because, as discussed earlier in the report, an increase in the minimum wage would boost economywide demand for goods and services and thereby generate an increase in the nation's total output and income. That additional income would raise federal taxes and lower benefits. By contrast, in the long term, and also as discussed earlier in the report, an increase in the minimum wage would generate a decrease in total output and income. That loss in income would lower federal taxes and raise benefits; those effects are incorporated in the discussion in the following section.

17. Congressional Budget Office, *Effective Marginal Tax Rates for Low- and Moderate-Income Workers* (November 2012), www.cbo.gov/publication/43709. Table 6 in that report shows an aggregate marginal rate for 2014 of 34.8 percent. Subtracting the marginal rate attributable to state income taxes yields a federal marginal rate of 32.2 percent. That rate includes the effects of federal income and payroll taxes and of refundable earned income, child, and premium assistance tax credits for health insurance purchased through exchanges. It also includes changes in benefits under SNAP and cost-sharing subsidies provided to some participants in health insurance exchanges. That report was published before the enactment of the American Taxpayer Relief Act of 2012, but CBO estimates that the average federal marginal rate for 2014 would remain at about 32 percent after incorporating the effects of that act.

18. The 12.4 percent Social Security portion of that tax is paid on earnings up to a threshold ($117,000 in 2014).

19. Some researchers have examined the change in cash and near-cash transfer payments that would result from a minimum-wage increase. See Linda Giannarelli, Kye Lippold, and Michael Martinez-Schiferl, *Reducing Poverty in Wisconsin: Analysis of the Community Advocates Public Policy Institute Policy Package* (Urban Institute, June 2012), http://tinyurl.com/q7jb8v6 (PDF, 2.1 MB); and Linda Giannarelli, Joyce Morton, and Laura Wheaton, *Estimating the Anti-Poverty Effects of Changes in Taxes and Benefits with the TRIM3 Microsimulation Model* (Urban Institute, April 2007), http://tinyurl.com/p75lejh (PDF, 2.9 MB). The authors estimate that the reduction in transfer payments for those receiving an increase in earnings would be roughly 4 percent of that increase in earnings.

20. A small portion of the premium assistance tax credits represents a reduction in revenues.

21. There would also be budgetary effects of some people's moving between eligibility categories for Medicaid and some people's moving between Medicaid and the Children's Health Insurance Program.

under current law and would receive higher earnings because of a minimum-wage increase would lose eligibility for Medicaid. Some of those people would gain eligibility for subsidized coverage through exchanges and would choose to take up that coverage; for those people, federal costs would rise. However, some of the people who would lose eligibility for Medicaid would not gain eligibility for subsidized coverage through exchanges (because their income would still be too low) or would gain eligibility but would choose not to take up that coverage (in part because they would have to pay a portion of their premiums themselves); for those people, federal costs would fall. Moreover, some people who, under current law, will not be eligible either for Medicaid or for subsidized coverage through exchanges (because they live in a state that has not expanded Medicaid coverage under the Affordable Care Act but will have too little income to qualify for the subsidies) would gain eligibility for subsidized coverage through exchanges and would choose to take up that coverage; for those people, federal costs would rise. The net federal cost of those various shifts would be small, CBO expects.

Effects for People Whose Income Would Fall

Apart from the group of workers whose earnings rose because of a minimum-wage increase, other people would generally see a reduction in real income, CBO estimates. Some of the reduction would consist of lower earnings for workers who became jobless for at least part of a year because of the change in policy. Some would consist of lower profits for business owners. The remainder would come from higher prices, which would reduce real income. However, it is unclear how much of the total reduction in income would come from each of those sources, and that allocation would affect the impact of a minimum-wage increase on the federal budget. CBO has not estimated the effective federal marginal tax rate for that collection of reductions in income, but the agency anticipates that it would probably be slightly smaller than the effective federal marginal tax rate for the people who would receive higher income.

CBO estimates that workers who were jobless for at least part of a year because of the minimum-wage increase would suffer a loss of real income. As a result, those workers would pay less in taxes and receive more in benefits. The effective federal marginal tax rate for those workers would be similar in magnitude to the rate for workers whose earnings rose.

CBO estimates that profits would also be lower. The lower profits would mean less in personal and corporate income tax receipts. CBO expects that some of the reduction in profits would be for businesses subject to the corporate tax, which would lower corporate tax receipts; the reduction in profits would also indirectly reduce personal income tax receipts, because stockholders' dividend income and realized capital gains on corporate stock would be lower. For those firms, CBO estimates that the decline in corporate and personal tax payments would amount to roughly one-third of the decline in profits. However, some of the reduction in profits would be for firms not subject to the corporate tax, most of whose income is directly subject to the individual income tax. For those firms, the resulting reduction in individual income tax payments could be somewhat lower, as a share of the reduction in profits, than the estimated one-third decline for firms subject to the corporate tax.

Prices would rise as a result of a minimum-wage increase, according to CBO's analysis. That increase in prices would raise federal transfer payments, because some of those payments, such as Social Security, are automatically indexed to changes in the price level. An increase in prices would also reduce federal personal income taxes, because many parameters of the tax system change automatically when the price level rises. Federal spending that is not subject to statutory caps and is not indexed to changes in the price level might also increase, although the extent of that increase would depend on the concentration of minimum-wage workers in the sectors of the economy in which the federal government was doing such spending. CBO was not able to estimate the effective marginal tax rate from the collection of changes in taxes and spending that would take place because of price changes.

Appendix A:
The Basis of CBO's Findings

This appendix describes the steps that the Congressional Budget Office (CBO) took to arrive at the estimates in this report—estimates of the number of low-wage workers affected by the two options for increasing the minimum wage; of the responsiveness of employment to changes in the minimum wage; of the options' total effects on employment; and of the options' effects on family income.

How CBO Estimated the Number of Workers Who Would Be Affected by the Options

CBO estimated the number of workers who would be directly affected by the two options for increasing the federal minimum wage. Directly affected workers are those whose wages would otherwise have been below the new federal minimum and who therefore would either receive a higher wage or become jobless if the new federal minimum was imposed. In 2016, CBO estimates, about 17.0 million workers would be directly affected by the $10.10 option and 7.7 million by the $9.00 option. CBO also estimated the number of workers whose wages would otherwise have been slightly above (as defined later in this section) the new federal minimum in 2016 and who would probably also be affected by a change in the minimum wage. Under the $10.10 option, there would be 8.0 million such workers; under the $9.00 option, 4.1 million. (The 33 million workers mentioned in the text—which refers to all workers who are projected to earn less than $11.50 under current law—includes not only the 17.0 million directly affected workers under the $10.10 option and the 8.0 million workers with wages slightly above $10.10 but also some workers, generally at the low end of that range, who are not covered by minimum-wage laws and some workers, at the high end of that range, who live in states projected to have high

minimum wages in 2016 and who therefore would probably not be affected by a change in the federal minimum.)

Of the 17.0 million workers directly affected by the $10.10 option, 16.5 million would end up with higher earnings during an average week in the second half of 2016, and 500,000 would end up jobless and therefore with lower earnings (as estimated using the approach described below). Of the 7.7 million workers directly affected by the $9.00 option, 7.6 million would end up with higher earnings during an average week in the second half of 2016, and 100,000 would end up jobless and therefore with lower earnings, according to CBO's estimate.

Workers Who Would Be Directly Affected by Increases in the Minimum Wage

CBO estimated the number of directly affected workers in three main steps: calculating the distribution of hourly wages in 2013; projecting the wage distribution in 2016 under current law; and identifying the workers who would be directly affected by a change in the federal minimum wage in 2016.

In the first step, CBO calculated hourly wages for all workers in calendar year 2013, using monthly data from the Census Bureau's Current Population Survey (CPS), which collects information from about 60,000 households. The CPS is designed to be representative of the U.S. civilian population as a whole; each observation in the survey represents a number of people, and that number is the observation's "sample weight." CBO used those sample weights to estimate effects for the entire population on the basis of the people who were surveyed. When respondents to the survey did not report an hourly wage, their hourly wages were calculated as their usual earnings per week divided by their usual hours worked per week.[1] Because calculated wages are subject to error, CBO adjusted those wages to be a weighted average of a worker's calculated wage and the average wage of workers with similar characteristics—increasing calculated wages that were below the group average and decreasing wages that were above it.[2]

In the second step, CBO applied forecasts of employment and wage growth to the hourly wages that it had calculated for 2013 to project the distribution of workers' hourly wages in 2016 under current law. CBO expects that very high-wage workers will experience faster wage growth in the next several years than will workers as a whole, so the forecast of wage growth for low-wage workers used in this analysis was smaller than the one in the agency's overall economic forecast. The forecast of wage growth also accounted for the penalties, imposed under the Affordable Care Act, that some employers will pay for not providing qualifying health insurance; those employers will probably pass along the cost of those penalties to their workers in the form of reduced wages.[3] In addition, CBO accounted for prospective increases in some states' minimum wages, including both changes scheduled in current state laws and changes projected on the basis of how states have changed their minimum wages in the past. That adjustment boosted projected wage growth for workers in those states. Altogether, CBO projected that nominal wages of low-wage workers—for example, those at the 10th percentile of the wage distribution—would grow at an average annual rate of 2.9 percent between 2013 and 2016 under current law.

In the third step, CBO identified workers who would be directly affected by a change in the federal minimum wage in 2016. That group includes most workers projected to have hourly wages lower than the new minimum. However, it does not include 2.6 million low-wage workers who, CBO projects, would not be covered or affected by the Fair Labor Standards Act (FLSA).[4] The group of directly affected workers does include 3.5 million workers who, though they may not be covered by the FLSA, are expected by CBO to be affected by an increase in the federal minimum because their hourly wages tend to be as concentrated near the minimum as are the wages of workers covered by the FLSA; those 3.5 million workers consist of employees of small firms, workers in occupations generally exempt from the FLSA, and teenagers in their first 90 days of employment.[5]

CBO distinguished tipped from nontipped workers because a separate minimum cash hourly wage applies to workers who receive more than $30 per month in tips. Under the FLSA and many state laws, employers may pay such workers a lower cash hourly wage if tips bring their total hourly earnings above the minimum hourly wage. To estimate the number of tipped workers, CBO applied the lower minimum cash wage to workers in 11 occupations (such as waiter, bartender, and hairdresser) whose compensation depends heavily on tips. They constitute about 10 percent of low-wage workers.

Other Workers Who Would Probably Be Affected by Increases in the Minimum Wage

CBO also considered the effects of a minimum-wage increase on the wages and employment of workers whose wages would otherwise have been higher than the new

---

1. If the number of hours that the respondents usually worked per week varied, CBO used the number of hours that they reported having worked during the week prior to the survey. If that number was unavailable, CBO used the average hours of full-time or part-time workers, as appropriate. If the Census Bureau imputed an hourly wage for the worker, CBO used that wage.

2. That adjustment is based in part on findings from Thomas Lemieux, "Increasing Residual Wage Inequality: Composition Effects, Noisy Data, or Rising Demand for Skill?" *American Economic Review*, vol. 96, no. 3 (June 2006), pp. 461–498, http://dx.doi.org/10.1257/aer.96.3.461.

3. See Congressional Budget Office, *The Budget and Economic Outlook: 2014 to 2024* (February 2014), Appendix C, www.cbo.gov/publication/45010. That forecast of wage growth was made in December 2013 and does not account for subsequent developments.

4. To project the percentage of low-wage workers who would not be covered or affected by the FLSA in 2016, CBO estimated the share earning less than the federal minimum wage (or their state's minimum wage, if higher) in 2013, which was 12 percent. Because the agency concluded that nontipped workers who reported being paid up to 25 cents less, and tipped workers who reported being paid up to 13 cents less, than the federal minimum wage—or the state minimum, if it was higher—had probably misreported their wages, it did not count such workers as being paid less than the minimum wage. The analysis does not account for localities' minimum wages because it uses data from the CPS, which does not identify the localities in which respondents work.

5. Department of Labor, "Wages and Hours Worked: Minimum Wage and Overtime Pay" (accessed January 23, 2014), www.dol.gov/compliance/guide/minwage.htm.

federal minimum in 2016. Those effects could be positive or negative for any particular worker, depending on whether that worker's value to a firm would be higher or lower if lower-wage workers became more expensive to employ. Available research, however, suggests that the average effect on the wages of those workers would be positive. (See Appendix B for a list of studies that CBO reviewed.)

In its analysis, CBO assumed that such "ripple effects" would probably apply to workers whose projected wage in 2016 was up to the amount that would result from an increase that was 50 percent larger than the increase in their effective minimum wage (incorporating both their state minimum and the new federal minimum) under either option. Thus, in states where the current minimum wage is $7.25, CBO anticipates that workers earning up to about $11.50 per hour would probably be affected by the $10.10 option. In states with a higher minimum wage, the ripple effect would be much smaller. For instance, under current California law, the minimum wage is scheduled to increase to $10.00 in 2016, and in that state, only workers earning up to $10.15 per hour would probably be affected by an increase to $10.10 in the federal minimum, by CBO's estimate.

Ripple effects added 8.0 million potentially affected workers to CBO's analysis under the $10.10 option and 4.1 million under the $9.00 option. Although CBO estimates that wage increases under the options are much more likely for those workers than for workers with still higher wages, the agency does not expect that all of them would receive wage increases. CBO did not have a basis for estimating the total number of workers whose earnings would rise, although that number would be less than the total number of potentially affected workers.

Uncertainty in the Estimates

Estimates of the total number of potentially affected workers are uncertain for at least four reasons. The first and most important is that, if CBO's forecast of wage growth for low-wage workers between 2013 and 2016 is either too high or too low, the result will be an underestimate or an overestimate, respectively, of the number of workers who would be directly affected by a change in the federal minimum wage. Second, determining whether workers are covered by the FLSA on the basis of what they report to the CPS yields inaccuracies. For instance, some respondents undoubtedly misreported their wages, earnings, or hours worked, leading CBO to classify some

unaffected workers as affected and vice versa; similarly, the use of occupation to classify people as tipped workers results in inaccuracies.[6] Third, changes in states' minimum wages could be different from what CBO projects. Fourth, the ripple effects could be smaller or larger than CBO projects.

How CBO Estimated the Responsiveness of Employment to Increases in Minimum Wages

CBO reviewed a large body of research to estimate how adopting either of the two options for increasing the minimum wage would affect employment. Such research typically calculates an employment elasticity—that is, the percentage change in employment induced by a percentage change in the minimum wage. Researchers have generally focused on the employment of workers with low average wages, such as teenagers, high school dropouts, and workers in low-wage industries. Initially focusing on estimates of the employment elasticity for teenagers (in part because they were the most commonly studied group), CBO arrived at a teen-employment elasticity for each of the options, after accounting for the fact that the $10.10 option differed significantly from the scenarios explored by prior research. CBO then synthesized the teen elasticities with broader research to construct elasticities for adults. (See Appendix B for a bibliography of the research that CBO reviewed.)

The elasticities discussed in this section would apply only to directly affected workers and not to others whose wages would be higher than the new minimum wages under the options. For example, CBO concluded that the $9.00 option probably would not affect the employment of workers who would earn more than $9.00 in 2016 under current law (except by increasing overall demand for goods and services, an effect discussed below). That conclusion was the result of considering two opposing factors. On the one hand, wages would probably increase for some of those workers (such as the supervisors of minimum-wage workers), as firms sought to maintain a differential between their wages and those of employees earning the minimum wage—and that wage increase

---

6. For a discussion of mismeasured wage rates, see, for example, John Bound, Charles Brown, and Nancy Mathiowetz, "Measurement Error in Survey Data," in James J. Heckman and Edward Leamer, eds., *Handbook of Econometrics*, vol. 5 (Elsevier, 2001), pp. 3705–3843, http://dx.doi.org/10.1016/S1573-4412(01)05012-7.

would tend to lower employment. On the other hand, some firms would probably employ more workers with wages higher than the new minimum, because the productivity of those workers relative to their wages would be higher than that of workers whose wages had been pushed up by the minimum-wage increase.

Elasticities for Teenagers Under the $9.00 Option

CBO reviewed the economic research to develop a range of estimates of the elasticity of teen employment with respect to a change in the minimum wage under the $9.00 option. On the basis of that review, CBO selected a central estimate of that elasticity of -0.075; in other words, a 10 percent increase in the minimum wage would reduce employment among teenage workers by three-quarters of one percent. However, there is considerable uncertainty about that elasticity, and CBO developed a range of estimates to reflect that uncertainty. The high end of the likely range was -0.15 and the low end was zero. In CBO's assessment, there is about a two-thirds chance that the effect of the $9.00 option on the employment of teenage workers would lie within that range. Some studies, however, have found that increases in the minimum wage raise employment slightly, while others have found much larger negative effects on employment than are reflected in CBO's range.

Several factors influenced CBO's conclusion about the range of elasticities for teenagers. First, CBO put more weight on studies using certain methodologies than on other studies. Several studies compare employment rates among states that have different minimum wages but otherwise similar labor markets; such analyses plausibly isolate the effects of minimum wages from the effects of national economic changes, such as fluctuations in the business cycle. Other studies try to isolate the employment effects of minimum-wage increases by comparing the national employment rate in years when the minimum wage was high to the rate in years when the minimum wage was low. CBO put the most weight on the studies of state-by-state differences, judging those studies to have estimated more accurately the effects of minimum wages on employment. Changes in state minimum wages are sometimes related to local economic conditions in ways that could lead elasticity estimates based on those changes to be higher or lower than the elasticity that would apply to similar changes in law in the future; CBO considered studies that took a variety of approaches to addressing that issue.

Second, CBO considered the role of publication bias in its analysis. Academic journals tend to publish studies whose reported effects can be distinguished from no effect with a sufficient degree of statistical precision. According to some analyses of the minimum-wage literature, an unexpectedly large number of studies report a negative effect on employment with a degree of precision just above conventional thresholds for publication. That would suggest that journals' failure to publish studies finding weak effects of minimum-wage changes on employment may have led to a published literature skewed toward stronger effects. CBO therefore located its range of plausible elasticities slightly closer to zero—that is, indicating a weaker effect on employment—than it would have otherwise.

Third, CBO considered whether economic conditions in 2016 could lead the responsiveness of employment to an increase in the minimum wage to be larger than it had been in the past. One recent study has found evidence that the employment elasticity is more negative when unemployment is high. However, CBO projects a national unemployment rate of about 6 percent for 2016—a rate similar to the average of unemployment rates during the periods studied in the literature from which CBO drew elasticity estimates.[7] CBO therefore did not adjust its central elasticity estimates to account for economic conditions in 2016.

However, the extent to which employment would respond to changes in the minimum wage in 2016 in the same way that it has in past years is uncertain. For example, the relatively slow growth in the wages of low-wage workers observed in the past few decades has been partly attributed by many analysts to growth in information and other technologies, which have automated some of the tasks traditionally done by those workers. Continued improvements in such technology will probably lead to the automation of some other tasks that they still perform, such as payment collection at retail stores. The pace of technological innovation, though, is difficult to predict. Uncertainty about future developments in the labor market is reflected in CBO's range of estimates.

---

7. See Congressional Budget Office, *The Budget and Economic Outlook: 2014 to 2024* (February 2014), www.cbo.gov/publication/45010. For additional information about CBO's projections of future labor market conditions, see Congressional Budget Office, *The Slow Recovery of the Labor Market* (February 2014), www.cbo.gov/publication/45011.

Elasticities for Teenagers Under the $10.10 Option

In analyzing the $10.10 option, CBO used a central estimate of the elasticity of employment for teenagers of -0.10, with a likely range from a very slight negative amount to -0.20. Four main factors differentiate the $10.10 option from the $9.00 option and from policies studied in previous research, leading CBO to conclude that the elasticity would be larger (in absolute value) under the $10.10 option.

First, the $10.10 option would index the minimum wage to inflation and would therefore result in a higher minimum wage for many years in the future. The federal minimum wage has not been previously indexed to inflation, and some employers may have refrained from reducing employment in response to prior minimum-wage increases, realizing that inflation would soon erode the cost of those increases. Therefore, an indexed minimum wage would probably reduce employment more than a nonindexed minimum wage would—and neither the $9.00 option nor most policies studied in past research are indexed.

Second, most studies measure changes in employment over a short term, typically a year or two. However, employment reductions after a minimum-wage increase are probably larger over a longer term, in part because those reductions may be less attributable to the elimination of existing low-wage jobs than to slower *growth* in the number of low-wage jobs, which is difficult to detect in short-term studies. CBO assessed the effects of both options in the second half of 2016—two years after the first step of the $10.10 option, but only one year after the first step of the $9.00 option. That longer lag between the initiation of the option and the evaluation date led CBO to estimate a larger elasticity for the $10.10 option than for the $9.00 option.

Third, raising the minimum wage from $7.25 to $10.10 represents a 39 percent increase, which would be larger than most of the increases that have been studied, and CBO expects that employment would be more responsive to a larger increase.[8] Many employers incur adjustment costs when they reduce staffing (especially if that requires restructuring their operations), which may deter them from laying off low-wage workers in response to a small increase in the minimum wage. But the savings from not having those employees are more likely to exceed the adjustment costs when the minimum-wage increase is large.[9]

Fourth, the $10.10 option would apply to a larger fraction of the workforce—one that accounts for about 10 percent of all hours worked, CBO projects—than many previous increases did. It would do so not only because the percentage increase is large, but also because the minimum wage before the increase would be higher in real (inflation-adjusted) terms than it was before many previous increases (see Figure 1 on page 5).[10] For example, although the percentage increase in the federal minimum wage from 2007 to 2009 was similar to the one projected under the $10.10 option, the fraction of the workforce affected under that option would be about five times as large (see Table A-1).[11] When a greater proportion of a firm's work hours are affected by the minimum wage, the adjustment cost per worker of reducing staffing (again, especially if the firm is restructuring its operations) is probably smaller, making the firm more likely to reduce employment.

Translating Elasticities From Previous Research for Use in CBO's Analysis

In order to project the change in employment that would result from the $9.00 and $10.10 options, CBO

8. The last increase in the federal minimum wage, implemented between 2007 and 2009, constituted a 41 percent increase, but earlier percentage increases were typically lower. Some states have implemented large percentage increases in the minimum wage, however. New York, for example, increased its minimum wage from $5.15 to $7.15 per hour—a 39 percent increase—between 2005 and 2007.

9. In addition, at the same time that the proposed increases in the minimum wage would take effect, the Affordable Care Act's requirement that many employers provide health insurance (or pay a penalty if they do not) will impose an additional cost on employers for some low-wage workers who do not currently have employment-based health insurance. CBO expects that the cost will ultimately be borne by workers through lower wages; but before that adjustment has fully taken effect, the cost further boosts the likelihood that employers' savings from reducing the size of their workforces would exceed their adjustment costs.

10. The 10 percent of work hours affected in 2016 by the $10.10 option is not directly comparable to the percentage of workers projected to make less than $10.10 per hour in 2016 as reported in Figure 1. That percentage is based on a count of workers, rather than of hours worked, and it includes workers making less than $10.10 who are not covered by the FLSA.

11. The 10 percent of work hours affected in 2016 by the $10.10 option reported above differs from the 11.4 percent in 2016 reported in Table A-1 mainly because of the different definition of directly affected workers used in Table A-1 to create a consistent series over time.

Table A-1.

Comparing Changes in the Federal Minimum Wage Since 1980 With Changes Under the Two Options

Year of the Minimum Wage Increase[a]	Percentage of Workers Earning Between the Old and New Minimum Wages	Percentage of Hours Worked by Workers Earning Between the Old and New Minimum Wages
Changes Since 1980		
1980	10.9	8.6
1981	11.7	9.2
1990	4.3	3.2
1991	5.2	4.0
1996	3.4	2.5
1997	5.8	4.3
2007	1.3	0.9
2008	1.9	1.4
2009	2.7	2.0
Average	**5.3**	**4.0**
Projected Changes Under the $9.00 Option[b]		
2015	3.9	2.3
2016	7.7	5.7
Average	**5.8**	**4.0**
Projected Changes Under the $10.10 Option[c]		
2014	6.3	4.7
2015	10.0	7.7
2016	14.1	11.4
Average	**10.1**	**7.9**

Source: Congressional Budget Office based on the Census Bureau's Current Population Survey and on data from the Department of Labor.

Note: For the analysis in this table, to create a consistent series over time, CBO focused on groups of workers earning between the old minimum wage and the new minimum wage that was scheduled to take effect within a year. To allow for some misreporting of wages, workers earning slightly below the old minimum wage were also included. The hours worked were those reported prior to the increase in the minimum wage. Those groups of workers differ from the groups of directly affected workers under the options discussed elsewhere in this report because they do not account for any wage growth, within the year prior to the new minimum wage's taking effect, that would have occurred if the minimum wage had not been raised, or for increases in state minimum wages that would have increased workers' wages during the period.

a. The amendments to the Fair Labor Standards Act of 1938 mandating the minimum wage increases for these years were enacted in 1977, 1989, 1996, and 2007.

b. The minimum wage would rise (in three steps, starting in 2014) to $10.10 by July 1, 2016, and then be indexed to inflation.

c. The minimum wage would rise (in two steps, starting in 2015) to $9.00 by July 1, 2016, and would not be subsequently indexed to inflation.

converted the elasticity estimates that it drew from the literature on teenage workers to elasticity estimates for directly affected teenagers and adults.

Elasticities for Directly Affected Teenagers. The research discussed above typically defines employment elasticity (e) as the responsiveness in the employment ($\%\Delta E$) of a group of workers, such as teenagers, to a change in the applicable minimum wage ($\%\Delta MW$ —that is, the

change in the federal or state minimum, whichever is higher), as shown in the following equation:

$$e_{literature} = \frac{\%\Delta E}{\%\Delta MW}$$

The elasticity ranges reported earlier in this appendix are based on that approach so that they will be more easily comparable to the elasticities typically reported in the research literature. In its calculations, however, CBO used elasticities that were modified in two ways to be more accurate estimates of the effect of the options.

The first modification that CBO made arose because the literature typically focuses on the historical employment response of *all* teenagers to a change in the minimum wage. Many of those teenagers initially had low wages and, when the minimum wage rose, received a wage increase (or were rendered jobless); but many other teenagers had wages that were higher than the new minimum and therefore were largely unaffected by the change. In contrast, CBO's approach examines the responsiveness of employment of only *directly affected* teenagers to a change in the minimum wage—that is, the responsiveness of employment of those who would otherwise earn less than the new minimum wage. When analyzing the $10.10 option, for example, CBO's approach focuses on the responsiveness of teenage workers who would have earned less than $10.10 per hour in 2016 if the option had not been implemented. The two approaches are similar, but they can yield different results when the fraction of teenagers with low wages varies over time and with policy changes. In CBO's view, an approach that focuses on the response of low-wage workers is more accurate.

The second modification that CBO made was to use elasticities that relate employment not to changes in the minimum wage itself but to average changes in workers' wages induced by a change in the minimum wage. (For instance, a worker who would otherwise have earned $9.00 per hour would receive a 12 percent increase if the minimum wage rose to $10.10. However, the minimum wage for that worker would rise from $7.25 to $10.10, an increase of 39 percent.) The elasticities that are typically reported in the literature are scaled to the increase in the minimum wage itself—but for two reasons, an approach relying on them is not as well suited for projecting the change in employment resulting from a future change in the minimum wage. First, that approach does not incorporate information about the distribution of workers' wages. For example, in a projection of the effect of the $10.10 option, it would make no difference, under that approach, whether most workers would otherwise have earned $7.25 or $10.09. Second, that approach regards all directly affected workers as equally likely to lose their jobs after a minimum-wage increase, no matter what they would otherwise have been paid. In CBO's view, by contrast, workers whose wages are just below the new minimum wage are more likely to remain employed after

it increases than workers who are earning substantially less and are probably less valuable to the employer. CBO's approach accounts for the distribution of workers' wages and for the difference in the likelihood of losing one's job.

CBO calculated the responsiveness of employment among directly affected teenagers by dividing the elasticities drawn from the literature by the portion of employed teenagers who would earn less than the new minimum wage before its implementation (p_{direct}) and then multiplying by the ratio of the percentage change in the applicable minimum wage ($\%\Delta MW$) to the average percentage change in the wages of those teenagers ($\%\Delta W_{direct}$).[12] The following equation shows the calculation:

$$e_{direct} \equiv \frac{\%\Delta E_{direct}}{\%\Delta W_{direct}} = \frac{e_{literature}}{p_{direct}} \times \frac{\%\Delta MW}{\%\Delta W_{direct}}$$

CBO calculated those conversion factors using CPS data from 1979 through 2009. The CPS data indicate that past increases in the minimum wage typically affected about a third of employed teenagers and were typically about 50 percent higher than the average of the wage changes necessary for compliance with the new minimum. Thus, elasticities for directly affected teenagers are about 4.5 times higher, CBO estimates, than the teen-employment elasticities with respect to the change in the applicable minimum wage discussed in the previous section.

Elasticities for Directly Affected Adults. Much less research has been conducted on the responsiveness of adult employment to minimum-wage increases than on the responsiveness of teenage employment. Using the available information, CBO concluded that the elasticity for directly affected adults was about one-third of the elasticity for directly affected teenagers, and the agency

---

12. A similar conversion was used in Charles Brown, "Minimum Wages, Employment, and the Distribution of Income," in Orley Ashenfelter and David Card, eds., *Handbook of Labor Economics*, vol. 3B (Elsevier, 1999), pp. 2101–2163, http://tinyurl.com/omxr3p7, and in David Neumark and William L. Wascher, *Minimum Wages* (MIT Press, 2008), http://mitpress.mit.edu/books/minimum-wages. The conversion relies on the assertion that the increase in the minimum wage does not have a net effect on employment for workers earning more than the new minimum wage. As discussed earlier, CBO concluded that the research supports that assertion, with the exception of the increase in employment that would result from greater overall demand for goods and services. The adjustment made to account for that increase in employment is discussed in the section "How CBO Estimated the Total Effects of the Options on Employment."

applied that proportional adjustment to the central estimates and likely ranges of elasticities for teens discussed above.

Some studies have found large elasticities for particular groups of adults, such as high school dropouts or African Americans in their 20s, but most of the adults who would be affected by the $9.00 and $10.10 options would not fall into those categories. A study that tracked directly affected adults regardless of their education, age, or race suggests that their employment is less sensitive to increases in the minimum wage than that of directly affected teenagers. One explanation for that lower degree of responsiveness is that employers facing an excess of workers or of job applicants tend to favor adults over teenagers. Supporting that explanation is research suggesting that encouraging employment among low-wage parents reduces employment among younger, childless adults.

CBO also reviewed studies that examined the response of employment to changes in the minimum wage for other groups of workers, such as those in particular industries. Those results were broadly consistent with CBO's findings for teenagers and adults after being adjusted to avoid apples-to-oranges comparisons. For example, several studies of the food and drink industry measured elasticities in terms of the change in all employment in the industry stemming from a change in the applicable minimum wage. Many of the employees at those businesses did not have wages low enough to be directly affected by a minimum-wage change; that factor largely accounts for differences between the smaller elasticities typically reported in studies of the food and drink industry and CBO's estimates of elasticities for directly affected workers.

How CBO Estimated the Total Effects of the Options on Employment

CBO's central estimates that the $10.10 and $9.00 options would reduce employment by roughly 500,000 and 100,000 workers, respectively, were based on four main factors. Two were discussed above: the number of low-wage workers directly affected by the options and the responsiveness of the employment of low-wage workers to increases in minimum wages. The remaining two factors were the change in the wages of directly affected workers and the increase in demand for goods and services caused by each option. To calculate the total effect on employment, CBO multiplied estimates of the first three factors together for teenagers; did the same for adults; added the results; and then added an amount to account for the fourth factor. To reflect the considerable uncertainty in estimating the total employment effect, CBO also reported a range within which, in the agency's assessment, there was about a two-thirds chance that the actual effect would lie.

The Increase in the Wages of Directly Affected Workers

CBO first projected wages for all workers in 2016 under current law; it then increased wages that would be below the new minimum wage under consideration to equal that new minimum. The difference between the directly affected workers' wages before and after that adjustment was used to calculate the average percentage changes in directly affected workers' wages (before accounting for job losses caused by the minimum-wage increase). Under the $10.10 option, CBO projects average percentage changes of about 18 percent for teenagers and 14 percent for adults. The projected changes are smaller under the $9.00 option—10 percent for teenagers and 8 percent for adults. All those percentage changes are lower than the percentage changes in the minimum wage itself because most low-wage workers in 2016 would earn more than $7.25 under current law.

The Increase in Demand for Goods and Services

Raising the minimum wage would have four direct effects on the aggregate demand for goods and services. First, consumption would be reduced among people who became jobless because of the minimum-wage increase. In estimating that effect, CBO accounted for lower savings and some borrowing by people who would thereby avoid a sharp reduction in their standard of living. Second, additional spending by affected workers with earnings increases would boost demand. Third, demand would be reduced because business owners and shareholders would absorb part of the cost of the minimum-wage increase in the form of reduced profits and therefore would reduce their spending. Fourth, demand would also be reduced because affected employers would pass part of their increased costs on to consumers in the form of higher prices for goods and services; those higher prices would reduce the average consumer's purchasing power, resulting in less spending by consumers after adjusting for inflation. (For examples of the research that CBO reviewed on these topics, see Appendix B.)

On balance, according to CBO's analysis, raising the minimum wage would increase demand for goods and services because, taken together, the second, third, and fourth direct effects would shift income from business owners and consumers (as a whole) to low-wage workers. Low-wage workers generally spend a larger share of each dollar they receive than the average business owner or consumer does; thus, when a dollar from business owners or consumers is shifted to low-wage workers, overall spending increases. The increase in demand from that shifting of income would be larger than the decrease in demand from the reduced consumption of people who became jobless, CBO estimates.

Increasing the minimum wage would also have indirect effects on demand that could either enhance or reduce the direct effects. For instance, the greater demand for goods and services just described would prompt some companies to increase investment to bolster their future production, further boosting demand. But higher prices of goods and services sold by companies employing minimum-wage workers would cause consumers to shift their purchases to other companies, potentially creating bottlenecks until those companies adjusted to the increased demand. On net, the indirect effects would reduce demand, according to CBO's central estimates. (Under current conditions, the indirect effects would increase demand, CBO estimates, but they would reduce demand in 2016 because the economy will be stronger and the Federal Reserve would therefore be more active in offsetting the direct increase in demand by raising interest rates.)

The increased demand for goods and services that would result from an increase in the minimum wage would have a short-term impact, boosting employment by a few tens of thousands of workers in the second half of 2016 under the $10.10 option, CBO estimates. The agency's estimation approach was similar to the one that it used to assess the effects of the American Recovery and Reinvestment Act of 2009 (ARRA) and of various policies designed to increase output and employment—but adjusted to account for the much stronger economy projected for late 2016.[13] Specifically, CBO estimated the impact of both the $10.10 option and the $9.00 option on demand while accounting for both the direct and indirect effects. Then CBO estimated the effect of those changes in demand on productivity, hours worked per worker, and employment, using historical relationships as a guide. Changes in demand would affect employment gradually,

over several quarters, because part of a rise in output would initially result in higher productivity and hours worked per worker, rather than in increased employment.

The overall increase in demand from boosting the minimum wage, and the resulting increase in employment, are represented in the findings of most previous research only to a small extent. For example, a study of impacts on directly affected workers captures the macroeconomic effects only on those workers, not on all workers. Also, a study of a minimum-wage increase in a given state may capture its effects on demand for in-state goods but not for out-of-state goods. After analyzing the importance of such factors, CBO concluded that previous research incorporated roughly 10 percent of the overall effects on aggregate demand. CBO therefore reduced its estimate of the economywide demand effects of a minimum-wage increase by about 10 percent to avoid double-counting those effects.

Uncertainty in the Estimates

CBO produced a range of estimates of the effect of increasing the minimum wage on employment by analyzing various sources of uncertainty. The three most important were the growth in wages of affected workers under current law over the next three years, the responsiveness of employment to changes in wages, and the extent to which an increase in aggregate demand because of higher labor earnings would increase employment. CBO concluded that two further sources of uncertainty—sampling variability in the CPS and the level of state minimum wages in 2016—were relatively insignificant.

To estimate a range of values for wage growth, CBO examined the history of wage growth rates and the extent to which those rates varied over three-year periods. To estimate a range for the responsiveness of employment to changes in wages, CBO used the elasticity ranges developed for the two options that were discussed above. CBO measured uncertainty in aggregate demand effects by

---

13. See Congressional Budget Office, *Estimated Impact of the American Recovery and Reinvestment Act on Employment and Economic Output From October 2012 Through December 2012* (February 2013), www.cbo.gov/publication/43945; and testimony of Douglas W. Elmendorf, Director, Congressional Budget Office, before the Senate Committee on the Budget, *Policies for Increasing Economic Growth and Employment in 2012 and 2013* (November 15, 2011), www.cbo.gov/publication/42717.

using methods similar to those that it used in its analysis of ARRA.[14]

Building on those ranges of wage growth, elasticities, and aggregate demand effects, CBO generated simulations of effects on employment that incorporated the likelihood that wage growth could be higher or lower by a certain amount, the likelihood that elasticities could be larger or smaller to a certain extent, and other sources of uncertainty. CBO used the results of those estimates to form a range for the effect on employment of each policy option. There is a two-thirds chance, in CBO's assessment, that the actual effects would be within the ranges reported.

How CBO Estimated the Effects of the Options on Family Income

CBO analyzed the effects on family income of the two options for increasing the federal minimum wage by comparing a projected distribution of family income in 2016 under current law with the distribution that would prevail if the federal minimum wage was increased to either $10.10 or $9.00. The monthly data from the CPS that CBO used in its analysis of employment did not contain the information on family income necessary for this analysis, so CBO instead used data from the CPS Annual Social and Economic Supplement (ASEC) that was administered in March 2013, which reported family income and individuals' earnings for calendar year 2012.

Wages and Family Income Under Current Law

Before it could estimate the effect of the two options on family income in 2016, CBO needed to project family income under current law. CBO used a two-step process similar to the one that it used in its employment analysis—first calculating hourly wages and annual family income in 2012 and then using those calculations to project wages and family income in 2016.

Hourly Wages and Annual Family Income in 2012.

CBO estimated the hourly wages of workers and annual income of families in 2012 by using data from the 2013

ASEC. Workers' hourly wages were calculated as their annual earnings divided by the number of hours they worked during the year (calculated as the number of hours they usually worked per week times the number of weeks they worked during the year).[15] As in its analysis of employment, CBO adjusted workers' calculated wages up or down to move their wage toward the average wage for workers with similar observable characteristics.

However, when CBO used those data to project workers' wages in 2016, it found far fewer workers who would be directly affected by the change in the minimum wage than it had in its analysis of employment.[16] The discrepancy probably arose because of greater measurement error in the ASEC than in the monthly CPS, which reports wages according to people's responses to a direct question about how much they earn per hour. CBO therefore further adjusted the distribution of hourly wages calculated from the ASEC to match more closely the analogous distribution from the monthly CPS, mostly by adjusting some workers' wages up to the minimum wage projected to apply to them in 2016 under current law.[17]

CBO also used the ASEC to measure the distribution of before-tax family cash income in 2012, which is the measure that the Census Bureau uses to determine the official poverty rate. That measure of income includes labor earnings, capital and business income, and other private sources of income, as well as cash transfers from the government, such as Supplemental Security Income (SSI) and Social Security (both Old-Age and Survivors

---

14. Felix Reichling and Charles Whalen, *Assessing the Short-Term Effects on Output of Changes in Federal Fiscal Policies*, Working Paper 2012-08 (Congressional Budget Office, May 2012), www.cbo.gov/publication/43278.

15. CBO did not exclude observations for which the Census Bureau imputed annual earnings, the number of hours of work per week, or the number of weeks worked per year.

16. To be consistent with the analysis of the number of workers affected by an increase in the minimum wage, CBO identified nontipped workers who were paid up to 25 cents less and tipped workers who were paid up to 13 cents less than the federal minimum wage—or the state minimum if it was higher—as workers who would be affected by a change in the minimum wage.

17. As it did in estimating the number of affected workers, CBO identified tipped workers as those in 11 occupations (such as waiter, bartender, and hairdresser) whose compensation depends heavily on tips. Throughout its analysis, CBO applied to those workers the lower minimum wage for tipped workers.

Insurance and Disability Insurance payments).[18] It does not include noncash government transfers, such as benefits provided through the Supplemental Nutrition Assistance Program (SNAP), Medicaid, or Medicare, nor does it reflect the taxes people pay or the tax credits they receive, such as the earned income tax credit (EITC).

Projecting Hourly Wages and Annual Family Income in 2016. CBO used the calculations described above and its forecasts of growth in wages and other income to project the distribution of hourly wages and annual family income in 2016.[19] As in the employment analysis, the forecast of wage growth used for this analysis was smaller than the agency's overall forecast of wage growth because CBO expects that very high-wage workers will experience faster wage growth in the next several years than other workers will.[20] In addition, CBO accounted for prospective increases in some states' minimum wages, including changes scheduled in current state laws and changes projected on the basis of how states have changed their minimum wages in the past.

To project family income in 2016, CBO used its forecasts of growth in the components of income when they were available—as they were for interest and dividends, for example. CBO projected that the other components of income will grow at the same rate that the price index for personal consumption expenditures does in CBO's forecast. CBO estimated that the number of workers will increase according to the agency's forecast of employment growth between 2013 and 2016. The rate of growth in the number of nonworking family members was similarly matched to the agency's forecasts of growth in the nonworking population.

---

18. Specifically, before-tax family cash income includes wage and salary earnings; pension or retirement income; income from self-employment, Temporary Assistance for Needy Families (TANF), Supplemental Security Income, Social Security, child support, unemployment compensation, workers' compensation, disability benefits, educational assistance, and financial assistance from outside the household; and other cash income.

19. See Congressional Budget Office, *The Budget and Economic Outlook: 2014 to 2024* (February 2014), www.cbo.gov/publication/45010.

20. In addition, the Affordable Care Act's requirement that many employers provide health insurance (or pay a penalty if they do not) will impose an additional cost on employers for some low-wage workers who do not currently have employment-based health insurance. CBO expects that the cost will ultimately be borne by workers through lower wages.

Estimating the Effects of Increases in the Minimum Wage on Family Income

The steps described above show how CBO formed an estimate of the distribution of hourly wages and family income in 2016 under current law. CBO then estimated how a higher minimum wage would affect family income in 2016. To do that, CBO first estimated the effect of an increase in the minimum wage on workers' annual earnings. CBO then projected how that change in earnings, along with several other factors, would change family income.

Changes in the Annual Earnings of Workers. CBO estimated the effect of increases in the minimum wage on the annual earnings of low-wage workers using methods similar to those used in its analysis of employment. The higher wages of two groups were multiplied by the workers' projected 2016 annual hours of work to estimate their annual earnings under the options. The first group consisted of workers who were projected to have wages lower than the new minimum in 2016 under current law. The second group consisted of workers whose projected wages in 2016 would be up to as much as $11.50; as in its analysis of the number of affected workers, CBO estimated that wages would rise for people in that category, on average.

The wages of the first group were initially adjusted up to the new minimum, and then further adjustments for ripple effects were made in both groups. Specifically, those ripple effects were projected to extend up to the amount that would result from an increase that was 50 percent larger than the increase in their applicable federal or state minimum wage under either option. Ripple effects were included for workers whose wages under current law were projected to be slightly less and slightly more than the minimum wages under each option, respectively. The ripple effects were the largest for workers who, under current law, would have earned precisely the minimum wage that would be set under the option. On average, the ripple effects were substantially smaller than the increases in wages needed to bring workers up to the new minimum.

CBO's analysis of annual earnings also accounted for reductions in employment—and therefore in some workers' earnings—that would result from the increases in the minimum wage. Here, CBO used the same employment elasticities that it used in its analysis of the options' effects on employment. Employment reductions were restricted to workers who would have had, under current law, an hourly wage less than the new minimum. Workers who would have had wages between the new minimum and $11.50 were not considered to be at risk of losing employment as a result of the minimum-wage increase, as discussed above.

The reductions in employment would be concentrated more among teenage workers than among older workers, CBO expects, both because they tend to have lower wages and because their employment typically responds more sharply to changes in the minimum wage (as discussed above). Among workers at least 20 years old, CBO anticipates that the reductions in employment would be disproportionately concentrated among those who would have had the lowest wages under current law (apart from those to whom the minimum wage would not apply). Because many low-wage workers move in and out of employment within a year, CBO estimated the effects of the employment loss among low-wage workers by assuming that the affected people worked, on average, about half as many weeks as they otherwise would have; CBO therefore lowered projected earnings by 50 percent for twice as many workers as the projected number of people who would become jobless (rather than lowering earnings by 100 percent for a number of workers equal to the number of people who would become jobless).

Changes in the Annual Income of Families. An increase in the minimum wage would not only affect family income by changing workers' earnings. It would also result in losses in income for business owners, decreases in real income for many people because of increases in prices, and increases in some people's income generated by higher demand for goods and services. To determine the economywide effect on total income, CBO subtracted the output lost because of the decline in employment from the output gained because of the increase in the aggregate demand for goods and services. On balance, the total amount of real income in the economy would increase by $2 billion in 2016 under the $10.10 option, CBO projects, and by $1 billion under the $9.00 option.

In CBO's estimation, overall real income would increase for families with income less than six times the poverty threshold but would decrease for higher-income families, because both the income losses for business owners and the increase in prices would have the greatest effects on those higher-income families. In CBO's estimation, about 1 percent of the reduction in real income from those two factors would fall on people living in families

whose income was below the poverty threshold, whereas about 70 percent would fall on people living in families whose income was more than six times the poverty threshold.

CBO used those estimates of the change in income for families to project how many families would move into and out of poverty.[21] Following the official definition of poverty, CBO did not consider the effects of a minimum-wage increase on taxes, tax credits, or noncash transfer payments in its calculations. (CBO has not analyzed the effects of minimum-wage increases on a measure of income that accounts for taxes, tax credits, or noncash transfers.) Some of those effects would partly offset the gain to families from a higher minimum wage. For example, workers who received higher wages because of an increase in the minimum wage would pay more payroll taxes (though they would later be eligible for more Social Security benefits), and some of their families would be eligible to receive less in noncash means-tested benefits, such as those provided by SNAP. The amount of the EITC received by workers in poor families would increase in some cases and decrease in others, depending on each worker's earnings and family income.

Uncertainty in the Estimates

There is considerable uncertainty about the effects of minimum-wage increases on family income. Some of the sources of uncertainty are the same as those in CBO's analysis of employment; they involve wage growth, the elasticity of employment with respect to the change in the minimum wage, and the magnitude of the macroeconomic response that would result from the redistribution of income. However, there are some additional sources of uncertainty in the analysis of the options' effects on family income. They include the following:

■ The effect on total income and on the income of families with different amounts of income is uncertain because of various factors, including how much spending varies by family income, the extent to which people avoid sharp changes in consumption when their income changes, the relative magnitudes of

---

21. The Census Bureau's poverty thresholds, which identify the income level below which families are classified as being in poverty, were projected to grow at the same rate that CBO forecast for growth in the consumer price index for urban consumers, or CPI-U. That approach is consistent with the fact that poverty thresholds are updated annually for inflation with the CPI-U.

profit reductions and price increases by firms paying increased wages, and the magnitude of indirect effects on demand.

■ It is uncertain how the reduction in employment resulting from a minimum-wage increase would be distributed among families during 2016. In its analysis, CBO distributed that employment reduction among families on the basis of the age and the wages under current law of the workers who live in those families. Alternative distributions would produce different effects on family income and poverty.

■ The effect of a higher minimum wage on the behavior of other people who live in low-wage workers' families is uncertain. For example, someone in that situation might work fewer hours in response to a spouse's higher earnings—or more hours, if the spouse lost employment as a result of the higher minimum wage. In general, such responses would probably offset to some extent the effects of the options on low-wage workers' family income.

Comparing CBO's Approach With Other Approaches

CBO's estimates of the effect of increasing the minimum wage on family income are based on a "simulation" approach.[22] That is, CBO estimated what the distribution of family income was likely to be in 2016 under current law and then projected how a higher minimum wage would alter that distribution by projecting

---

22. Also, CBO's analysis of income focuses on *family* income, in part because that is how official poverty measures are determined. Some analysts, however, have focused on *households* as the unit over which income is shared. CBO expects that the results using that alternative measure would yield qualitatively similar results, in this instance.

wages and employment (and then earnings and family income). CBO then projected the effect on the poverty rate by comparing each family's poverty status under current law with its poverty status under the two options.

An alternative approach to forecasting the effect of a minimum-wage increase on poverty rates is to estimate the historical correlation between the poverty rate and the minimum wage and to use that correlation to project a change in the poverty rate for a given change in the minimum wage. Some of the estimates produced by studies taking that approach would imply that the $10.10 policy would reduce poverty by more than CBO has estimated. (See Appendix B for examples of such studies.)

There are several reasons that the two approaches may yield different results. It might be, for example, that CBO's analysis underestimates the increase in income that would accrue to poor families if the minimum wage was increased. That underestimate might occur if the minimum wage raised earnings for workers projected to have wages above the new minimum by more than CBO has estimated. It might also be that an increase in the minimum wage would alter family structure—through increased marriage rates, for example—in ways that reduced the number of families whose income was below the poverty threshold; such effects would be captured in the historical correlation approach but not in CBO's simulation approach. Alternatively, the effect on poverty of a minimum-wage increase might vary over time—for example, if the number of low-wage workers in families with income near the poverty threshold varied over time. If that was true, the correlation analysis might be less informative than CBO's simulation method, which uses more current data.

Appendix B:
Research About the Effects of Minimum-Wage Increases

To develop its estimates of the effects of minimum-wage increases on employment and family income, the Congressional Budget Office (CBO) drew on the following research.

Reviews of Research About Employment Effects

For studies that analyze the central tendency of other studies' estimates of employment effects, accounting for journals' tendency to publish studies that find significant effects, see Dale Belman and Paul Wolfson, "Does Employment Respond to the Minimum Wage? A Meta-Analysis of Recent Studies From the New Minimum Wage Research," in *What Does the Minimum Wage Do?* (Upjohn Institute, forthcoming), http://tinyurl.com/p475ahg (PDF, 224 KB);

Hristos Doucouliagos and T. D. Stanley, "Publication Selection Bias in Minimum-Wage Research? A Meta-Regression Analysis," *British Journal of Industrial Relations*, vol. 47, no. 2 (June 2009), pp. 406–428, http://dx.doi.org/10.1111/j.1467-8543.2009.00723.x; and

David Card and Alan B. Krueger, "Time-Series Minimum-Wage Studies: A Meta-Analysis," *American Economic Review: Papers and Proceedings*, vol. 85, no. 2 (May 1995), pp. 238–243, www.jstor.org/stable/2117925.

For reviews that examine the methods and data used in the research literature that estimates employment effects of the minimum wage, see Sylvia Allegretto and others, *Credible Research Designs for Minimum Wage Studies*,

Discussion Paper 7638 (Institute for the Study of Labor, September 2013), http://tinyurl.com/ld9rwmg; and

David Neumark and William L. Wascher, "Minimum Wages and Employment," *Foundations and Trends in Microeconomics*, vol. 3, no. 1–2 (March 2007), pp. 1–182, http://tinyurl.com/o7cngec.

For a review of the literature on the effect of Britain's minimum wage (which was introduced in 1999), see Low Pay Commission, *National Minimum Wage*, Report 2013 (April 2013), Chapter 2, pp. 19–74, http://tinyurl.com/m6bbe93.

For a review of the literature on mechanisms that might explain small employment effects, see John Schmitt, *Why Does the Minimum Wage Have No Discernible Effect on Employment?* (Center for Economic and Policy Research, February 2013), http://tinyurl.com/b54lk8m.

For a literature review that covers a variety of effects, including the effects found in other countries, see David Neumark and William L. Wascher, *Minimum Wages* (MIT Press, 2008), http://mitpress.mit.edu/books/minimum-wages.

For reviews of that book, see Arindrajit Dube, "*Minimum Wages*. By David Neumark and William L. Wascher," *Journal of Economic Literature*, vol. 49, no. 3 (September 2011), http://dx.doi.org/10.1257/jel.49.3.719.r18; and

Richard V. Burkhauser, "*Minimum Wages*. By David Neumark and William L. Wascher," *Industrial and Labor Relations Review*, vol. 64, no. 1 (September 2010), pp. 202–203, http://tinyurl.com/o3gy5bg.

For a review of the research literature before 1999, see Charles Brown, "Minimum Wages, Employment, and the Distribution of Income," in Orley C. Ashenfelter and David Card, eds., *Handbook of Labor Economics*, vol. 3, part B (Elsevier, 1999), pp. 2101–2163, http://tinyurl.com/mmkdrme.

For an early review of the literature from an international perspective, see Organisation for Economic Co-operation and Development, "Making the Most of the Minimum: Statutory Minimum Wages, Employment and Poverty," in *OECD Employment Outlook 1998—Towards an Employment-Centred Social Policy* (OECD Directorate for Labour and Social Affairs, June 1998), Chapter 2, http://tinyurl.com/q6rs9a2.

For an early review of the new minimum-wage research from the first half of the 1990s, see David Card and Alan B. Krueger, *Myth and Measurement: The New Economics of the Minimum Wage* (Princeton University Press, 1995), http://press.princeton.edu/titles/5632.html.

For a very early review of the literature, see Charles Brown, Curtis Gilroy, and Andrew Kohen, "The Effect of the Minimum Wage on Employment and Unemployment," *Journal of Economic Literature*, vol. 20, no. 2 (June 1982), pp. 487–528, www.jstor.org/stable/2724487.

Other Research About Employment Effects

CBO also considered the following studies, which are generally too recent to have been covered by the reviews listed above.

For studies focused on employment among teenagers, see Laura Giuliano, "Minimum Wage Effects on Employment, Substitution, and the Teenage Labor Supply: Evidence From Personnel Data," *Journal of Labor Economics*, vol. 31, no. 1 (January 2013), pp. 155–194, http://dx.doi.org/10.1086/666921;

Yusuf Soner Baskaya and Yona Rubinstein, "Using Federal Minimum Wages to Identify the Impact of Minimum Wages on Employment and Earnings Across the U.S. States" (draft, Department of Economics Workshop, University of Chicago, December 2012), http://tinyurl.com/lmjohgl (PDF, 580 KB); and

Sylvia A. Allegretto, Arindrajit Dube, and Michael Reich, "Do Minimum Wages Really Reduce Teen Employment? Accounting for Heterogeneity and Selectivity in State Panel Data," *Industrial Relations*, vol. 50, no. 2 (April 2011), pp. 205–240, http://dx.doi.org/10.1111/j.1468-232X.2011.00634.x.

For a recent study that focuses on how the effects of minimum-wage increases vary with economic conditions, see John T. Addison, McKinley L. Blackburn, and Chad D. Cotti, "Minimum Wage Increases in a Recessionary Environment," *Labour Economics*, vol. 23 (August 2013), pp. 30–39, http://dx.doi.org/10.1016/j.labeco.2013.02.004.

For analyses of changes in employment in industries where low wages are prevalent, see William E. Even and David A. Macpherson, "The Effect of the Tipped Minimum Wage on Employees in the U.S. Restaurant Industry," *Southern Economic Journal*, vol. 80, no. 3 (January 2014), pp. 633–655, http://tinyurl.com/kv6fz6c;

Jonathan Meer and Jeremy West, *Effects of the Minimum Wage on Employment Dynamics* (draft, Texas A&M University, December 2013), http://tinyurl.com/cllro5p (PDF, 2.9 MB).

Arindrajit Dube, *Minimum Wages and Aggregate Job Growth: Causal Effect or Statistical Artifact?* Discussion Paper 7674 (Institute for the Study of Labor, October 2013), http://tinyurl.com/kx6t2yz;

David Neumark, J. M. Ian Salas, and William Wascher, *Revisiting the Minimum Wage-Employment Debate: Throwing Out the Baby With the Bathwater?* Working Paper 18681 (National Bureau of Economic Research, January 2013), www.nber.org/papers/w18681;

John T. Addison, McKinley L. Blackburn, and Chad D. Cotti, "The Effect of Minimum Wages on Labour Market Outcomes: County-Level Estimates from the Restaurant-and-Bar Sector," *British Journal of Industrial Relations*, vol. 50, no. 3 (September 2012), pp. 412–435, http://tinyurl.com/ot9apya; and

Arindrajit Dube, T. William Lester, and Michael Reich, "Minimum Wage Effects Across State Borders: Estimates Using Contiguous Counties," *Review of Economics and Statistics*, vol. 92, no. 4 (November 2010), pp. 945–964, http://dx.doi.org/10.1162/rest_a_00039.

For recent studies that examine changes in employment among a variety of groups that earn low wages, on average, see Arindrajit Dube, T. William Lester, and Michael Reich, *Minimum Wage Shocks, Employment Flows and Labor Market Frictions*, Working Paper 149-13 (Institute for Research on Labor and Employment, June 2013), www.irle.berkeley.edu/workingpapers/149-13.pdf (3.4 MB); and

Joseph J. Sabia, Richard V. Burkhauser, and Benjamin Hansen, "Are the Effects of Minimum Wage Increases Always Small? New Evidence From a Case Study of New York State," *Industrial and Labor Relations Review*, vol. 65, no. 2 (April 2012), pp. 350–376, http://tinyurl.com/mn566b3.

For examples of earlier studies about effects on adults with low wages, see David Neumark, Mark Schweitzer, and William Wascher, "Minimum Wage Effects Throughout the Wage Distribution," *Journal of Human Resources*, vol. 39, no. 2 (Spring 2004), pp. 425–450, http://tinyurl.com/ncgswlg;

David Neumark, "The Employment Effects of Minimum Wages: Evidence From a Prespecified Research Design," *Industrial Relations*, vol. 40, no. 1 (January 2001), pp. 121–144, http://dx.doi.org/10.1111/0019-8676.00199;

Richard V. Burkhauser, Kenneth A. Couch, and David C. Wittenburg, "Who Minimum Wage Increases Bite: An Analysis Using Monthly Data From the SIPP and the CPS," *Southern Economic Journal*, vol. 67, no. 1 (July 2000), pp. 16–40, www.jstor.org/stable/1061611; and

Donald Deere, Kevin M. Murphy, and Finis Welch, "Employment and the 1990–1991 Minimum-Wage Hike," *American Economic Review*, vol. 85, no. 2 (May 1995), pp. 232–237, www.jstor.org/stable/2117924.

For examples of research on the long-term effects of changes in minimum wages, see Isaac Sorkin, "Are There Long-Run Effects of the Minimum Wage?" (draft, University of Michigan, October 2013), https://sites.google.com/site/isaacsorkin/papers;

Dale L. Belman and Paul Wolfson, "The Effect of Legislated Minimum Wage Increases on Employment and Hours: A Dynamic Analysis," *Labour*, vol. 24, no. 1 (March 2010), pp. 1–25, http://tinyurl.com/nhp7mth; and

Michael Baker, Dwayne Benjamin, and Shuchita Stanger, "The Highs and Lows of the Minimum Wage Effect: A Time-Series Cross-Section Study of the Canadian Law," *Journal of Labor Economics*, vol. 17, no. 2 (April 1999), pp. 318–350, http://dx.doi.org/10.1086/209923.

For a reexamination of earlier research using time series methods, see Nicolas Williams and Jeffrey A. Mills, "The Minimum Wage and Teenage Employment: Evidence From Time Series," *Applied Economics*, vol. 33, no. 3 (February 2001), pp. 285–300, http://dx.doi.org/10.1080/00036840122088.

Research About Family Income Effects

For analysis of the effects of minimum-wage changes on family income and the poverty rate, see Joseph J. Sabia and Robert B. Nielsen, "Minimum Wages, Poverty, and Material Hardship: New Evidence From the SIPP," *Review of Economics of the Household* (January 2013), http://dx.doi.org/10.1007/s11150-012-9171-8;

Arindrajit Dube, "Minimum Wages and the Distribution of Family Incomes" (draft, University of Massachusetts, Amherst, December 2013), http://tinyurl.com/muab8nc (PDF, 1.52 MB);

David Neumark and William Wascher, "Does a Higher Minimum Wage Enhance the Effectiveness of the Earned Income Tax Credit?" *Industrial and Labor Relations Review*, vol. 64, no. 4 (July 2011), pp. 712–746, http://tinyurl.com/looy95w;

Joseph J. Sabia and Richard V. Burkhauser, "Minimum Wages and Poverty: Will a $9.50 Federal Minimum Wage Really Help the Working Poor?" *Southern Economic Journal*, vol. 76, no. 3 (January 2010), pp. 592–623, http://dx.doi.org/10.4284/sej.2010.76.3.592;

Joseph J. Sabia, "Minimum Wages and the Economic Well-Being of Single Mothers," *Journal of Policy Analysis and Management*, vol. 27, no. 4 (Autumn 2008), pp. 848–866, http://dx.doi.org/10.1002/pam.20379;

Robert H. DeFina, "The Impact of State Minimum Wages on Child Poverty in Female-Headed Families," *Journal of Poverty*, vol. 12, no. 2 (October 2008), pp. 155–174, http://dx.doi.org/10.1080/10875540801973542;

Richard V. Burkhauser and Joseph J. Sabia, "The Effectiveness of Minimum-Wage Increases in Reducing Poverty: Past, Present, and Future," *Contemporary Economic Policy*, vol. 25, no. 2 (April 2007), pp. 262–281, http://dx.doi.org/10.1111/j.1465-7287.2006.00045.x;

Congressional Budget Office, *Response to a Request by Senator Grassley About the Effects of Increasing the Federal Minimum Wage Versus Expanding the Earned Income Tax Credit* (attachment to a letter to the Honorable Charles E. Grassley, January 9, 2007), www.cbo.gov/publication/18281;

David Neumark, Mark Schweitzer, and William Wascher, "Minimum Wage Effects Throughout the Wage Distribution," *Journal of Human Resources*, vol. 39, no. 2 (Spring 2004), pp. 425–450, http://tinyurl.com/ncgswlg;

Craig Gundersen and James P. Ziliak, "Poverty and Macroeconomic Performance Across Space, Race, and Family Structure," *Demography*, vol. 41, no. 1 (February 2004), pp. 61–86, http://dx.doi.org/10.1353/dem.2004.0004;

David Neumark and William Wascher, "Do Minimum Wages Fight Poverty?" *Economic Inquiry*, vol. 40, no. 3 (July 2002), pp. 315–333, http://dx.doi.org/10.1093/ei/40.3.315;

David R. Morgan and Kenneth Kickham, "Children in Poverty: Do State Policies Matter?" *Social Science Quarterly*, vol. 82, no. 3 (September 2001), pp. 478–493, http://dx.doi.org/10.1111/0038-4941.00037;

Lonnie K. Stevans and David N. Sessions, "Minimum Wage Policy and Poverty in the United States," *International Review of Applied Economics*, vol. 15, no. 1 (2001), pp. 65–75, http://dx.doi.org/10.1080/02692170120013358;

John T. Addison and McKinley L. Blackburn, "Minimum Wages and Poverty," *Industrial and Labor Relations Review*, vol. 52, no. 3 (April 1999), pp. 393–409, www.jstor.org/stable/2525141; and

David Card and Alan B. Krueger, *Myth and Measurement: The New Economics of the Minimum Wage* (Princeton University Press, 1995), http://press.princeton.edu/titles/5632.html.

For related analyses of wage and employment spillovers from increases in minimum wages, see David Lee and Emmanuel Saez, "Optimal Minimum Wage Policy in Competitive Labor Markets," *Journal of Public Economics*, vol. 96, no. 9–10 (October 2012), pp. 739–749, http://dx.doi.org/10.1016/j.jpubeco.2012.06.001;

Joseph J. Sabia, Richard V. Burkhauser, and Benjamin Hansen, "Are the Effects of Minimum Wage Increases Always Small? New Evidence From a Case Study of New York State," *Industrial and Labor Relations Review*, vol. 65, no. 2 (April 2012), pp. 350–376, http://tinyurl.com/mn566b3;

David H. Autor, Alan Manning, and Christopher L. Smith, "The Contribution of the Minimum Wage to U.S. Wage Inequality Over Three Decades: A Reassessment," Working Paper 16533 (National Bureau of Economic Research, November 2010), www.nber.org/papers/w16533;

David Lee, "Wage Inequality in the United States During the 1980s: Rising Dispersion or Falling Minimum Wage?" *Quarterly Journal of Economics*, vol. 114, no. 3 (August 1999), http://qje.oxfordjournals.org/content/114/3.toc; and

Charles Brown, "Minimum Wage Laws: Are They Overrated?" *Journal of Economic Perspectives*, vol. 2, no. 3 (Summer 1988), pp. 133–145, http://dx.doi.org/10.1257/jep.2.3.133.

Research About Other Effects

For research about consumption and price effects, see Daniel Aaronson, Sumit Agarwal, and Eric French, *The Spending and Debt Responses to Minimum Wage Increases*, Working Paper 2007-23 (Federal Reserve Bank of Chicago, revised February 2011), http://tinyurl.com/7z5sgcc;

Daniel Aaronson, "Price Pass-Through and the Minimum Wage," *Review of Economics and Statistics*, vol. 83, no. 1 (February 2001), pp. 158–169, http://dx.doi.org/10.1162/003465301750160126; and

David Card and Alan Krueger, *Myth and Measurement* (Princeton University Press, 1995), http://press.princeton.edu/titles/5632.html.

For a review of the literature on the implications of technological change for low-wage workers, see Daron Acemoglu and David Autor, "Skills, Tasks and Technologies: Implications for Employment and Earnings," in David Card and Orley C. Ashenfelter, eds., *Handbook of Labor Economics*, vol. 4, part B (Elsevier, 2011), pp. 1043–1171, http://dx.doi.org/10.1016/S0169-7218(11)02410-5.

For research about fringe-benefit effects, see Brooks Pierce, "Recent Trends in Compensation Inequality," in Katharine G. Abraham, James R. Spletzer, and Michael Harper, eds., *Labor in the New Economy* (University of Chicago Press, 2010), pp. 63–98, http://papers.nber.org/books/abra08-1;

Kosali Ilayperuma Simon and Robert Kaestner, "Do Minimum Wages Affect Non-Wage Job Attributes? Evidence on Fringe Benefits," *Industrial and Labor Relations Review*, vol. 58, no. 1 (October 2004), pp. 52–70, http://tinyurl.com/o8lrxjh; and

Masanori Hashimoto, "Minimum Wage Effects on Training on the Job," *American Economic Review*, vol. 72, no. 5 (December 1982), pp. 1070–1087, www.jstor.org/stable/1812023.

List of Tables and Figures

Tables

Figures

About This Document

This Congressional Budget Office (CBO) report was prepared in response to interest expressed by a number of Members of Congress. In keeping with CBO's mandate to provide objective, impartial analysis, the report contains no recommendations.

Nabeel Alsalam, William Carrington, Molly Dahl, and Justin Falk prepared the report, with contributions from Sarah Masi, Benjamin Page, Felix Reichling, Robert Stewart, and David Weiner and with guidance from Joseph Kile. Christina Hawley Anthony, Sheila Campbell, Wendy Edelberg, Peter Fontaine, Heidi Golding, Patrice Gordon, Edward Harris, Chung Kim, Joyce Manchester, Alexandra Minicozzi, Damien Moore, Sam Papenfuss, Jonathan Schwabish, Chad Shirley, and Rebecca Verreau of CBO provided helpful comments. Charles Brown of the University of Michigan, Richard Burkhauser of Cornell University, Harry Holzer of Georgetown University, Lawrence Katz of Harvard University, Alan Krueger of Princeton University, Casey Mulligan of the University of Chicago, and William Wascher of the staff of the Board of Governors of the Federal Reserve System provided comments about CBO's analytical approach. (The assistance of external reviewers implies no responsibility for the final product, which rests solely with CBO.)

Jeffrey Kling and Robert Sunshine reviewed the report, Benjamin Plotinsky edited it, and Jeanine Rees prepared it for publication. The report is available on the agency's website (www.cbo.gov/publication/ 44995).

Douglas W. Elmendorf
Director

February 2014

www.ingramcontent.com/pod-product-compliance
Lightning Source LLC
Chambersburg PA
CBHW080619180526
45168CB00007B/2974